There Is Gold in the Golden Years

But Sometimes You Have to Dig for It

Mary Jean Teachman

For more information about this title or to order other books
and/or electronic media, contact the publisher:

Atkins & Greenspan Publishing
18530 Mack Avenue, Suite 166
Grosse Pointe Farms, MI 48236
www.TwoSistersWriting.com

ISBN:
ISBN 978-1-956879-10-0 (Hardcover)
ISBN 978-1-956879-09-4 (Paperback)
ISBN 978-1-956879-11-7 (eBook)

Printed in the United States of America

All the stories in this work are true.

Cover and Interior design: Van-garde Imagery

To my wonderful husband, Dr. Gerard Teachman, and our children, family members, and friends.

You've all played a part in my life's journey.

My daughter passed away while I was finishing this book. She was in a terrible car accident. No mother should lose her child. It's not supposed to happen. People tell me there is nothing more tragic than losing a child. But I found out there is and that's losing two children.

The pain at times is unbearable and I can't believe it will stop. She will never walk through our door again. I will not see her again.

I hope that I will someday be able to laugh again and to love my life again, but it will take time. I'll keep talking to her, even though I won't hear her answers. And I will keep loving her until I join her.

Valarie was diagnosed with bipolar disorder in her early twenties and she was on medications and received therapies her entire life. Although she experienced some bipolar episodes that required hospitalizations, she never gave up. She used those experiences to enhance her ability to continue her life-long mission of helping others, which was almost a spiritual calling. If she saw someone in need, she offered help without ever considering her own needs.

Everyone who knew Valarie loved her. No one has said a negative word about her. We received many cards from friends who sent their condolences. All of the cards and messages emphasized how kind, loving, and generous she was.

These words were sent to us by one of her high school friends: "I have been all around this great big world and I have seen all kinds of girls, but your daughter was like a holy woman. Her beauty stands alone."

Contents

Why I Wrote This Book

The ship arrives in the harbor. She blows her horn to let people know that she has arrived. She's been on a long, hard journey, and she's finally home. She's brought her goods to the people. Some run with excitement to the pier; others walk leisurely. But they all get there in the end.

I've been on a journey to find peace, joy, and happiness. I've gone about it in my own way, and it took a long time for me to get to this point. I will continue seeking peace, joy, and happiness, as there is never too much of it. One day, my ship will arrive for me, and I will get on board and know that a new adventure will begin...

I'm writing this book through the eyes of a 90-year-old woman. I want to show how my life has changed throughout the years and the joy I experience at my current age. I live a productive and fulfilling life, and I'm grateful for that. I don't want to be younger. In fact, I'm happy with the aging process and find contentment in it. Being older in years doesn't mean that life has lost its value. In fact, there is *more* value. All of our lives change throughout our lifetimes as we move along on our individual paths.

I also want to dispel the idea that this is the time of life to be in a state of fear or worry. Age is only a number; it's not a punishment. Trials and tribulations can strike at any time. All of life's stages are different… the beginning, the middle, and the later years. Many people look at getting older as a minus, but I dispute that notion. I just see it as a plus.

I am not *old*. To be old is to be worn out. I'm simply in another stage of life. A tree grows from an acorn. The acorn gestates in the ground. Eventually a sprig pops up and says "Hello" by its presence—just as a baby cries upon being born.

Spring has always been my favorite season. The trees are growing new lime-green leaves. The birds appear. Flowers emerge from the ground. The tiny yellow bird goes into the small round hole of the birdhouse, deposits the twigs that are in its mouth, and flies out again. Mr. and Mrs. Bird have a lot of work to do. They're going to be a family soon, and they're preparing their home.

I had to get my home ready for new thinking. I picked up twigs of compassion, acceptance, and nonjudgment, and deposited them into my heart to welcome an abundance of love. The twigs were wet in the spring, dry in the summer, different twines of color in the fall, and brittle in the winter. I gathered them all and embraced them. They are permanent residents in my heart.

I've reached an age that brings more depth to my life. I look back and see that I've shed old emotions, wants, and desires. I have a different awareness. The path that I've traveled is one I will always remember fondly, but it is my life *now* that brings me the greatest happiness because I've discovered things about myself that I never knew existed.

I realize that family, friends, nature, kindness, love, and acceptance reign now. I appreciate nature more. Mother Earth is so giving, and Her bounty is endless. I look at the trees and their beauty. How long did it take them to get to their height? I don't know for sure, but I do know they help us by filtering the air we breathe. The flowers bring us such beauty. We should bow to nature. It is there for us to enjoy.

I recently woke up one morning and had the realization that my time on this planet is not unlimited. Of course, I've always been aware of that reality, but on that particular day, it hit me like an avalanche. However, I reflected upon it, and all of a sudden, a wave of happiness enveloped me. I want to enjoy *every* moment of life and cherish it. It's not as if I haven't appreciated my time in this universe; I just never dared to completely accept my mortality. We all leave. It's only a matter of when and under what circumstances. It is the final surprise.

This age has its perks. I find pleasure in being able to do what I want to do and not be on a strict time schedule. I can go to sleep and get up when I want to, meditate as long as I wish, and choose to stay home or go out. My husband, Gerry, and I have lunch dates instead of dinner dates, because we like to relax at home in the evening and go to bed early.

We like to take long walks, go on vacations whenever we choose to, and work in our garden. In other words, we have the freedom to do what we want, when we want to. Today is truly what is important, no matter what age we are. This moment is to be lived. I grab on to it. Life has challenges; that's part of being here.

And I don't know how long my life will continue, but I'm looking forward to celebrating my 100th birthday in nine years.

I realize that each day is one to be cherished. I'm incredibly happy that my husband, Gerry, and I have a loving, caring relationship. I'm also so grateful for our children: Forrest, who has left this planet; Valarie, who recently joined her brother; Robert; and Jonathan and his wife, Carolyn. I love my other family members so much, too, including: my brother, Jim, and his wife, Maida; my sister-in-law, Jan; and my nieces, nephews, and friends, who are like family.

The birthdays ending in zeros, including the glorious 100, seem to have more meaning than the others. One supposedly reaches maturity on one's twenty-first birthday, but I've learned something different with the passing years, primarily about myself. I don't believe in looking back and yearning to be a younger age. Each age has its positives and negatives. I look for the pluses at every period of life. I have a clarity about people and the world that I didn't have when I was younger. Life has taught me well.

Different decades have their own particular challenges, but my motto has always been, "Never give up." I've tried to maintain a positive attitude during difficult times, but some days have been harder than others. There are lessons in the experiences that I've had, and I'm here to learn from them. However, sometimes I ask the universe, "Can you give me a hint, please?"

I wonder what the common denominator is among all of us. Is it the capacity to love, hate, survive, self-destruct, cry, attack, help, or ignore? I know that love plays a huge role in all of this. I believe that if we come from love—love for ourselves and others— the world will have better energy. We are beings with a spiritual nature. We may not like others' lifestyles, but we can accept them as equal human beings. Unfortunately, many of us judge people by how much money they have, the color of their skin, and their religion. Our differences should not define us. We are all human beings—the same species. That is our commonality. It's only common sense to acknowledge this.

I know that life can be tough. It's a roller-coaster ride from beginning to end, and it can be bumpy or smooth. I never imagined that I would be 90. I suppose that's not completely accurate. I just didn't think about it. We're all on different trains, but our starts and stops are different. That doesn't mean that we can't empathize with each other. We can accept our differences for what they are—not bad or good, just different.

I've found out that I can be a valuable member of society at 90, probably even more so, because of what I've learned on the road of life. I want to continue to grow as long as I'm here. I know that it's a privilege to reach this age, and at times I almost can't believe that I made it. I look at it as only a number. I don't know what I expected, but I'm glad it is what it is. Acceptance about life is vital to living with happiness.

There *is* gold in the golden years! Spiritual growth and enhanced awareness allow us to accept the changes in our bodies, and even enhance our ability to enjoy deeper pleasures. Aging brings us wisdom, and with it, the recognition that few things frighten or intimidate us, and even fewer things impress us. We gain a deeper understanding of the meaning of truth and beauty. Sometimes we have to dig deep to find it, but it's there. It's like finding gold in a mine. It can be difficult to find, but the nuggets can yield great happiness.

Father Time marches on. I know that the clock is ticking, and I'm willing to walk to the beat. Instead of longing for days that are gone, I live each day fully. I used to think that being young was where it was at. Sure, youth has its benefits, but being older is a gift, too. We need to appreciate all of the stages of our lives.

In the entire scheme of things, life is quite a short journey, so I don't want to waste one precious moment. I'm near the end of my road, but I still have miles to go. I'm full of wonder and curiosity. What will happen next? I don't know, but whatever happens, I look forward to it and will treasure every minute of this trip.

An oak tree has been steadfast and growing for years. It bends with the wind, changes its leaves in the fall, sheds them in the winter, and grows new ones in the spring. I can rely on that old oak tree. Its shade in the summer keeps me cool. The color of its leaves in the autumn is a thing of beauty, and new lives in the spring signal that winter is over, and the long-awaited summer is here.

I call myself an oak tree. I can rely on myself. I see beauty in the world, and I have eternal hope for all the seasons. The old oak tree was born like that, but I wasn't. I've been fortunate to achieve it. I found it by shedding my leaves: old thoughts and patterns of living. I came forth with new ones by developing new perspectives. I can still bend with the wind, shed the old, and grow new ones. It's up to me.

Life is a series of adventures that are both rewarding and challenging. My book is based on that premise; it's about the different ways in which the Golden Years can be rewarding. I've tried to be as honest as my memory has allowed me to be. I've lived my life with passion, love, and kindness. Have I made mistakes? *Yes!* Do I regret them? *Yes!* I just don't dwell on them.

I hope my words resonate with you, and that they guide you on your journey through this experience we call... *life*.

CHAPTER 1

My Grandmother

Younger people don't see the experiences that older individuals have had. Many times, they just see old people. They don't realize that elders have gone through the same emotions that they have, as well as the same trials and tribulations. No matter what age we are, we're all human, with the same basic feelings.

Some of us are older, and some of us are younger. Hopefully the older generations have learned many lessons throughout their lives, and they have a better perception of the way things are. That is the walk of life. Our knowledge and experiences can change us for the better. No one is ever too old to learn. Times change and so do we—it is the rhythm of life! Younger people may feel that aging means falling apart, but I believe that, in many ways, we're getting better as we age.

"No, no! I don't want to go to America. I want to stay here in Ireland with my brothers and sisters. I'll never see you again. I love you. Please, please let me stay!"

My grandmother, Lizzie, my mother's mother, was sent to America from Ireland during the potato famine in the late 1800s.

Her sister was tagged to go, but she eloped so that she could stay in Ireland. My grandmother was told that she had to take her sister's place. She was heartbroken and didn't want to leave. My grandmother begged to stay at home, but to no avail. Her parents were desperate. They were incredibly poor and needed one less mouth to feed. It's interesting to note that not one of her brothers had to leave their home. My grandmother had to make the sacrifice. Her parents insisted that she go, and she simply had no choice.

So, at the age of fifteen, Lizzie left Molehill, Ireland, a small town about thirty minutes from Dublin. She took the train to the dock, boarded the boat, and sailed to America. Up until then, she'd only been as far as Cloone Village, where her parents came from. And now she was going to cross the sea by herself into unknown territory. She was a strong girl, and she did what she had to do. She didn't have the luxury of feeling sorry for herself.

I have no idea what the journey entailed. Maybe the seas were rough, and she got seasick. The loneliness and the stark reality that she would probably never see her family again had to be devastating. She'd never been away from them, and she was close to her older brother. Would they ever meet again? What were her thoughts? She must have felt great despair and sorrow. I can only imagine how difficult it was for her.

After a long journey from Ireland to the United States of America, she finally arrived at her destination: Boston, Massachusetts. The priest who was supposed to meet her wasn't there. What was she feeling at that moment? My grandmother was in a land where nothing was familiar, so she was probably terrified. Finally, after an hour of waiting, he arrived. I can only imagine her relief upon seeing him. She got into his car, and he drove her to the house of the family she was scheduled to work for. Apparently, they were kind and generous people. She worked for them as their maid. I'm not sure how long she was employed by them, but she was as happy as she could be, under the circumstances.

I'm amazed when I think about her strength, and her ability to adapt to a completely new situation. What a remarkable woman! She's an example of being strong and doing what she had to do. She had to forge ahead because that was the only option. She was a tiny woman, about 5'2" tall, with a head of very curly, light-brown hair, and very small size two feet. She used to get shoes for a pittance because they were samples. Her small feet came in handy.

Eventually, her three sisters, Bridget, Mary, and Julia, came to America. Mary lived in Chicago, Bridget lived in Texas, and Julia lived in New York. I only met Aunt Mary. I didn't know the other two, but I was told that Aunt Julia danced in the Ziegfeld Follies. They had productions on Broadway from 1897 until 1931. The Follies girls were lavished with jewels, flowers, and other tokens. I assume that happened to Aunt Julia, because she married a member of the Waterman Pen company. They all had lives that were very different from my grandmother.

My grandmother met my grandfather, Oscar, who resided in New Bedford, Massachusetts. I don't know the circumstances of their meeting, but he courted her for seven months, and then they got married in 1900. I regret that I didn't ask my grandmother what her life was like back then. I'm aware that at that time she couldn't call her parents. She wrote letters that took a long time to arrive in Ireland, and it took the same amount of time to get a reply from her family. Life was so different then—no TV, no cell phones, no computers, no airplanes, no FaceTime. That was more than 120 years ago.

Here are some of the events that were taking place around that time:

- President William McKinley was assassinated, and Theodore Roosevelt became president.

- In 1901, the first east/west radio broadcast was made from the United States to England. Radio was in its infancy.

- The first union was formed.

- The first teddy bear arrived in the USA.

- The Martha Washington Hotel, the first hotel exclusively for women, opened in New York City.

- The first World Series took place.

- The first box of crayons with eight colors sold for five cents.

- Ford Motor Company was founded in 1903.

My grandfather, Oscar, was an interesting man. He was a determined individual who overcame many obstacles. Physically, he was 5'5" tall with a full head of brown hair. He had an Eastern accent and maintained it his entire life. He had difficulty getting work in Boston, so a friend in Cincinnati, Ohio, who worked for a salvaging company, wrote and told him that he could get him a job where he worked.

My grandparents packed up their meager belongings and took the train to Cincinnati. The train had luxurious cars, but because of the small amount of money they had, they were in the least comfortable section. That was okay. They were young, in love, and happy to leave Boston. They were going to a city where my grandfather could provide an income for the two of them.

They found accommodations in a boardinghouse. There wasn't much space in their new home, but at least they had a place to live. It was similar to their home in Boston. Their first child arrived in 1905: my mother, Isabelle Margaret Gerard.

My grandfather got a job working in a mill, which was tedious and backbreaking. After three years, he couldn't imagine living his life like that forever. He heard that Piqua, Ohio—which is located in southern Ohio, about eighty-five miles from Cincinnati—was hiring men to work. So, he and my grandmother packed up their belongings and took the train to Piqua. The town was named after a clan of Shawnee Indians and is located along the banks of the Great Miami River. One had to cross a bridge to get into the city.

White people could easily cross that bridge into Piqua, but people of color could not. They lived in a small section outside of town. They had to get permission to go over that bridge, with a white man guiding them. The vocal quartet known as The Mills Brothers lived there. On Saturday nights, they would cross over the bridge with a priest and sing for a small amount of money. They couldn't go by themselves. That was part of the injustice at that time, and an example of the barbaric fashion in which people of color were treated.

My grandfather's first job was menial, but he eventually secured a position of substance and became quite successful in real estate later on in his life. He also donated his time at Christmas to the Salvation Army. He played a banjo while sitting out in the cold to collect money for them.

Early in their marriage, my grandmother did the laundry for some families in town. My mother had to pick it up and deliver it after dark, because of my grandmother's pride. She was ashamed that they were so poor at that time. It could be easy for me to ask:

"Why would she feel like that?"

Sometimes it's hard to really understand what someone is going through, but I do understand. The Irish immigrants were discriminated against at that time in history. They were treated like some of our immigrants are treated today. They were not viewed as equals. Some of the people in our culture select certain groups of people and brand them as unworthy. We're supposed to all be equal, but unfortunately that's not how it was then, and often not how it is today.

We always loved to visit my grandparents, because it was so much fun. My mother had three sisters. Jeanette, the second-born sister, was quiet and sweet, with a head of fluffy, brown curls. She had a beautiful, operatic voice and loved to sing. Rosealice, the youngest, was pretty, with a lovely figure and straight, brown hair. She loved playing the piano and dancing. My mother, the firstborn, was full of energy and made everyone aware that she was the oldest. She also had a nice figure and brown hair. She didn't have a good singing voice, but she chimed in anyway. Margarette was the fourth born. We all sang to music and danced. It's still one of my favorite things to do, and back then, it was magical to me.

My mother had three brothers: John, her favorite, was third in line. He was quite tall, and loved to swear and drink beer. He always took the bus from Piqua to Detroit, which was a long ride, to visit my brothers and attend my graduations. I loved him for that. Walter was fifth in line, average in height, and also really liked his beer. All of them had Irish blood in them. Unfortunately, he would leave for four or five days at a time to cater to his drinking habit.

My Uncle Joe was sixth in line, about 5'6" tall, and very interesting. He was the mystical one, believing that we could converse with the other side. I went to one of his séances at his home in Florida, and it was fascinating. There were six people in attendance: three females and three males. I'd never met two of the men, but they were quite friendly. I was very comfortable sitting in a chair and waiting for a spirit to arrive to talk to Uncle Joe. After we'd been there for about five minutes, a spirit came in and gave messages through my uncle to another person attending the séance. That man understood who was talking and was thrilled to hear what he had to say. I was fascinated. I had dabbled a bit in spirituality, but this session really piqued my interest.

That's when I embarked on a path to find a new way of living via the spiritual world. I now believe in reincarnation and that I'm here for a purpose. Actually, this belief has brought me great comfort. I've learned that there's a reason why we suffer great sorrows, and I've come to accept them. I don't expect anyone to believe the same things I do, though. I honor everyone's individual beliefs.

My grandmother was a fabulous cook and prepared sumptuous dinners. My cousins and brothers and I collected fireflies at night, which abundantly lit up the sky and made it magical. We played with complete abandonment. I particularly looked forward to the morning. I could smell the fragrance of coffee brewing in the kitchen. To this day, I associate the smell of coffee with my grandparents' home.

My grandfather definitely ran their household. He also enjoyed his cigars. I picture him with a cigar in his mouth most of the time. He would visit us in Michigan and it was wonderful. Grandpa would take us out to get ice cream or just take us for a ride in his old car. I loved him very much.

I found out later in life that he was a philanderer and had a series of girlfriends. I think my grandmother knew about them, but didn't admit it. It was hardly a secret, because Piqua is such a small town. He was sixty-two years old when he died instantly of a cerebral hemorrhage. He was climbing out of the window of his girlfriend's house when her husband came home early. It was only a matter of time until my grandmother found out the circumstances of his death.

Eventually, she did learn the lurid details, and she never got over the humiliation. I can only imagine the anguish she felt. She was hurt and angry. Her family tried to keep the truth from her, but in a small town, gossip flies like a tornado. She probably didn't want to be seen at church or walking down the street, because she knew that people were aware of what had happened.

Life became unbearable for her. She latched onto whiskey to block out the nightmare she was experiencing. She developed diabetes, but still continued to drink. I suppose it was a refuge for her. She probably wasn't strong enough to keep going forward, so alcohol was her friend. She must have suffered so much at that time of her life. I just wanted to give her love. I don't think we should criticize people who are experiencing anguish of any kind. In fact, I don't think we should *ever* criticize others.

My mom, dad, and I went to Piqua to visit my grandmother many times. I was sixteen years old the last time I saw her. I climbed the stairs to her bedroom with a heavy heart. She was ill and bedridden, and I could see that tiny, little body with the head full of white hair against the pillows. I felt so sorry for her. I'd never seen my grandmother sick. We started talking, and in the middle of our conversation, she begged:

"Mary Jean, please get me the bottle of whiskey that's in the closet. Please!"

I was so conflicted. I'll never forget how my grandmother was pleading with me. No one else would help her, so I was in turmoil. I knew what I was supposed to do, but I also realized her anguish. Of course, I *did* retrieve the bottle, and I don't regret it because it alleviated her pain for a while.

One month later, my grandmother struggled to get out of bed to go downstairs. She fell while walking down the steps and died instantly. Her agony was gone. I felt the relief that she must have experienced. My grandmother's journey on this planet was finally complete, and I was happy for her. I remember her funeral like it was yesterday. She was laid out at home, which was typical for that time.

The priest from the local parish, St. Mary's, came to the house that first night and blessed my grandmother, which was a ritual in the Catholic faith at that time. The next evening, I stayed up all night guarding the casket with my mother's youngest sister, Rosealice.

It was a surreal experience, as darkness descended upon us. There were no stars in the sky, and no moon, so it was very dark. I was mesmerized, as my beloved grandmother's body was before my eyes the entire night. It took time, but I eventually adjusted to it. I got to really know Aunt Rosealice that evening, and, in that respect, the experience was amazing. We talked all night. Since I was just sixteen, her primary advice was:

"You can marry a rich man just as easily as a poor one."

I wasn't thinking of getting married at that time, but she wanted me to remember that message.

Aunt Rosealice had experienced misfortune in her life and was suffering financially back then. Her first husband had been physically cruel. I remember being at my grandparents' home, and my aunt and her husband were there for the day. I was four years old, and my six-year-old brother, Tom, and I were alone in the room with my aunt and uncle. All of a sudden, her husband hit her, and little Tom stood up and kicked him in the leg. "Don't hit my aunt!" Tom ordered.

My uncle was stunned that a small child would defend her in that way, so he didn't hit her again, at least not then and there. I don't know what happened after that, but she did get a divorce a couple of years afterward. I can only imagine what must have transpired.

Then Aunt Rosealice met her second husband, Andy, who was tall, dark, and handsome. He courted her, and she fell in love with him. He was very dapper and drove a beautiful convertible with a rumble seat. The year was 1941, and I was ten years old. My aunt lived with my grandparents at that time. Andy would bring presents to Aunt Rosealice's children, Mary Ann and Judy, and me. Then he would take us for a ride with the top down. We never wanted it to end. We looked forward to those afternoons so much. I was included because it was summer and I was spending time at my grandparents' home. I felt like a princess.

My Aunt Rosealice and Andy were so in love, so they got married. They had two sons and were very happy. After five years, my aunt found out that Andy was running around with other women.

She confronted him, and he vowed that he'd stop. Unfortunately, that never happened. She was heartbroken and eventually got a divorce. Money was very scarce, but she was able to buy a home and turn it into a boardinghouse. She worked extremely hard until her death, but never complained. I now understand why she gave me the message about whom I should marry. Her life would have been so much easier if she'd accumulated some savings.

I don't know if my grandfather truly loved my grandmother. I believe she loved him, and they did live together until his death. They had seven children who lived, and they lost three children at birth. When their lives ended, they had thirty-five grandchildren. I can see by the threads of her life that my grandmother had immense character. I loved and admired her for that.

Years ago, when the Irish had wakes after the deaths of their loved ones and people came to offer their condolences, they were served food and beverages. The body was laid out on a bed in the person's own home, with rosary beads entwined in his or her crossed hands. Flowers and candles were usually placed about the casket. The laid-out corpse always had somebody standing beside it. This was mainly out of respect for the deceased individual. Many years earlier, in Ireland, the casket had to be guarded to prevent body snatchers from grabbing the corpse, as the robbers could sell it to make money. How gruesome.

I was taught by my church that true happiness was found in heaven, and only by enduring the world was that possible. Knowledge of my mortality has caused me to recognize that life on this earth is to be lived passionately and to its fullest—not sacrificed for some future reward.

CHAPTER 2

My Parents

One day, if you're lucky, you'll be your parents' age. You will constantly change throughout your life, and awareness will cause you to awaken to new experiences—some good and some not so good. People have walked the road before you. They will walk it after you.

Farther down the road, your psyche, wants, needs, and desires will change. Please remember that your parents have already walked down this road, and you will understand them better as you age. Maybe their desires and ways of living were different, but they have definitely traveled that road. As you're walking yours, be kind and generous with your love and attention.

My mother and father met in Piqua, Ohio. My mother lived in Piqua, and my dad lived in Sidney, which is about ten miles north of Piqua. At the age of seventeen, my mother would go to the local dance hall every Saturday night. Her parents insisted that she take her younger brother and two sisters with her, and if she refused, then she couldn't go. She loved dancing, so she brought her sisters, Jeanette and Margarette, and her brother, John, along. She would put on her favorite dress, apply lipstick, brush her brown, shiny hair, grab her two sisters and brother, and run out the door. She would drive her father's car, and they would all chug along to the dance hall.

My father had been going to this same dance hall for some time. The very first time he saw my mother, he knew he wanted to meet her. It took some time, but finally, one night, he summoned up the courage to ask her to dance. He had rhythm and was a very good dancer. She agreed because she'd seen him dance and liked what she saw. He immediately fell in love with her and courted her with a passion. It wasn't so instantaneous for her, though. A friend told her that my father was three years younger than she was. That presented a huge obstacle for her, as she didn't want to be with a younger man. Apparently, women rarely did that at the time. But these days, it's different. (My husband is seven years younger than I am, and I like it!)

One Saturday night, after another fun evening had ended and the dance hall closed, my mother and her siblings got into her parents' car and turned on the ignition, but it wouldn't start. She didn't know what to do. My father was in his car and saw that she was having trouble, so he offered to help. She was happy that he wanted to be of assistance, so she thanked him. He went to his car and pulled out a long, heavy rope. He then tied it to the front bumper of *her* car and tied the other end to the back bumper of *his* car. He started his car, which immediately pulled away, but my mother's car didn't budge.

The reason was that he hadn't tied the rope tightly, because he wanted to be alone with her. My mother was furious and insisted that he immediately take her back to her car. Of course, he did. He then tied the rope securely and drove my mother, her younger brother, and two sisters to their home. That seemed to be the turning point in their relationship. My mother recognized how much he cared for her, and she realized that she had strong feelings for him as well. It didn't hurt that he was successful. They became engaged after dating for six months.

Because my mother was Irish Catholic, religion was more important to her than it was to my father. He hadn't been raised in a religious family. I'm not sure my mother would have married him if he hadn't converted to the Catholic religion. I'm just thankful that he did, because he was such a wonderful father.

After their engagement, my father moved to Detroit for five months. He had to get a job, as there were none in Piqua or Sidney. Fortunately, he got one in a factory in Detroit. Life was so different then. My dad toiled for twelve hours a day doing very hard work. Even though some days he would come home with his hands bleeding, he never complained. He knew that if he did, he'd be fired. There were no unions then.

On April 13th, 1929, the day before their marriage, my dad took the bus from Detroit to Piqua. On April 14th, they had a lovely ceremony, surrounded by their families. There was a small reception after their vows were taken. I have pictures from their wedding, and I love looking at them. My mother is in her wedding dress with a beautiful veil on, which I still have, and my father looks so handsome in his suit. It's difficult for me to think of my parents being younger, making mistakes, and living life like all young people do. It just doesn't fit into the picture I have, although I know that they had the same wants and needs as any young people. First and foremost, I can't help but think of them as my parents.

A few hours later, after their wedding, they boarded a bus to Detroit to start their life together. There were tears of joy and sadness. They had each other, but they knew they wouldn't see their family often. My mother was pleased when they arrived in Detroit, the largest place she'd ever been. "I saw so much beauty," she later told me. "The streets were full of trees, the sun was shining, and the people were friendly."

Detroit was incorporated as a town in 1802 and as a city in 1815. In the 1920s, it grew faster than most American cities. It was called "Dynamic Detroit," because of the growth of the auto industry. It was also called the "Automobile Capital."

Many people, particularly people of color, left the South to start new lives in Detroit. There was still prejudice, but at least there were opportunities for work. Unfortunately, minorities were limited to where they could live. Their neighborhood was called the Black Bottom. New migrants from the South arrived daily to seek employment in the automobile industry. It's hard to look back and see how a group of people were limited in their opportunities simply because of their color.

There was a notorious gang in Detroit at the time called the Purple Gang. They were made up of a mob of men who were bootleggers and hijackers. They got their start in the Hastings Street neighborhood, known as Paradise Valley on Detroit's Lower East Side. By the 1920s, during Prohibition, Detroit had become a major port for running and selling alcohol products from Canada. The runs were made by night in boats crossing the Detroit River, particularly on very dark nights when there was no full moon shining.

Bootlegging netted the Purple Gang millions of dollars, but the mob was also involved in extortion, hijacking, and jewelry thefts. After the repeal of Prohibition in the 1930s, the Purple Gang members joined the growing national crime syndicate that was replacing the old-school Mafia leadership, fondly known as the Mustache Petes.

My father had rented a small flat on Ellery Street, right off East Grand Boulevard near downtown Detroit. He worked for Packard Motors. I'm not sure how long he worked there, but he left that job to work at Chrysler, because he was offered a higher salary. My parents settled in and began their new life together. Money was tight, but they were happy. My mother adjusted to not being with her family, even though she couldn't speak to them because she and my father couldn't afford a phone. At that time, many people were in the same situation. She corresponded with her loved ones by letter. It took a while for mail to get back and forth, but the wait was worth it.

All of a sudden, out of the blue, the stock market crashed on October 24th, 1929. It happened on what became known as "Black Thursday," which was the beginning of the Great Depression. Unemployment reached twenty-five percent, and people committed suicide, many by jumping out of windows, because they'd lost all their money. There were long lines of people on the street begging for food. They were happy to just get an apple. My parents felt like the lucky ones, because my father was bringing in an income. But then he, too, lost his job. However, he was fortunate to quickly find a job selling coffee and other items on a coffee route in downtown Detroit. The days were long, the work was hard, and the pay was meager, but he and my mother were able to eat, and they were grateful that they had a place to live.

The Depression caused many farmers to lose their farms. At the same time, years of overcultivation and a drought created the

"Dust Bowl" in the Midwest. It marked the end of agriculture in a previously fertile region. Thousands of these farmers and other unemployed workers looked for work in California. Many ended up living as homeless "hobos." Others moved to shantytowns called "Hoovervilles," named after then-President Herbert Hoover. My father also wanted to start over in California, but my mother was against moving there, so they stayed in Detroit. The times were turbulent, but they survived. However, America as a whole was in chaos.

Nevertheless, my parents decided to start their family. My brother Tom was born on February 17th, 1930. I was born on June 27th, 1931. My brother Jack was born on October 12th, 1932. My brother Kyle was born on October 9th, 1935, and my brother Jim was born on December 10th, 1941.

Did I mention that my mother was Irish Catholic and my father was a convert?

CHAPTER 3

My Brothers

Life presents many obstacles. A sprinter jumps high into the air, and many times, he or she wins the contest. I feel that we have to jump over many obstacles and handle what we can. Life is different for all of us. We don't have to win contests. We are on our individual journeys. Our roads go in different directions. That doesn't mean that we have to get and stay lost. We can always find our way.

I had four brothers, and I loved them all. Tom was special to me because he always protected me. He was smart, kind, honest, 6'3" tall, and movie-star handsome. I always knew I could rely on him. When I was three years old and Tom was four and a half, he didn't like the way my mother was treating me, so he decided to take me to a safer place. He put me in his little red wagon and set off on our way. Where? He wasn't sure, but that didn't matter.

Tom didn't know it at the time, but our dad was keeping track of us. He followed us, but didn't let us see him. After a short period of time, Dad finally approached Tom and convinced him that our mother wouldn't hit me again. Tom then agreed to take me back to our home. How could I not love someone who protected me like he did? I felt that assurance my entire life. I was keenly aware that I was safe, even if our father hadn't followed us. Today it's so different. Parents have to keep track of their children all the time. Life was simpler then.

Tom was born in a hospital; the rest of us weren't. My parents found out that it was too costly for my mother to go to the hospital to deliver, so my other brothers and I were born at home. My mother became pregnant with me when Tom was six months old. She had difficult pregnancies and was sick a good deal of the time. It had to be terribly hard to have a six-month-old and be pregnant and not feeling well.

On June 27th, 1931, it was apparent that I was on my way. It was two o'clock in the morning, and my parents didn't have a phone in their house, so my dad quickly ran to make a call on a phone located on the street corner. Dr. Kyle Townsend answered and said:

"Go home, time the contractions, and then call me back."

My father did exactly that. He ran back home again, checked on the timing of the contractions, ran back to the phone, and called Dr. Townsend again.

"Please hurry," my father said. "The contractions are two minutes apart."

"I'm on my way." He immediately left for our home.

Dad ran in the door, out of breath, and there I was, on the bed, kicking my feet and waving my arms, ready to face the world. My father was stunned, but jumped into action and wrapped a blanket around me. He held my mother's hand, trying to reassure her that all would end well. Dr. Townsend didn't get there for ninety minutes, because he had a difficult time finding an open gas station, and his car was about to run out of gas.

Consequently, the cord wasn't cut for an hour and a half. Today, some doctors say that it's beneficial not to cut the umbilical cord immediately, because it delivers more blood to the brain. The American College of Obstetricians and Gynecologists is the latest major medical organization to recommend that. I consider myself lucky. Generally, I've had good health. Who knows, maybe that's part of the reason. Whatever the case, that was how I began my life journey.

I wasn't around to witness my oldest brother Tom's birth, and I don't recall the birth of my brother Jack, as I was only fifteen months old. However, I was four years old when my brother Kyle was born, and I remember it vividly. I woke up on the morning of October 9th, 1935, and heard voices in my parents' bedroom, which was the next bedroom over. Tom, Jack, and I slept in the same room, as there were only two bedrooms in our home. I got out of bed, dressed, went to my parents' door, knocked on it, and asked to enter. I was always curious about what was going on. My grandmother, my dad's mom, came out.

"Mary Jean," she said, "go downstairs right now, and I'll make breakfast for you."

I ate my breakfast, but all the while, I was aware that something unusual was going on in my parents' bedroom.

Finally, my grandmother went upstairs, and the coast was clear. What luck. I had a plan, and I could now carry it out. I was determined to climb the telephone pole, or the tree situated right outside of my parents' room. I assessed the situation and decided I would climb the pole, and then I could look through the window and see what was happening. I stood at the bottom of the pole, looked up at the spikes on which I could put my feet, and decided to embark on my mission. I reached the first spike, then proceeded with my right foot and then my left. I was making progress.

All of a sudden, my heart started beating so hard I thought it would jump out of my chest. *Danger!* There were wires overhead. How could I avoid them? I had to climb between them to see into the window. Suddenly, I heard:

"Mary Jean, Mary Jean, get down off that tree right now!"

I looked down, and there stood my grandmother with her hands on her hips. I was saved. I scampered down the pole and was relieved that she'd come outside at that moment. "You have a new baby brother," she said.

I found out that my brother Kyle had entered the world in my parents' bedroom. He was a cute little guy, and I fell in love with him at first sight. He was full of energy and let us know that he was here. I helped to take care of him. I remember a few of the times that I was told to watch him, I would put him up in a tree and then I could go off and play with Tom and Jack. I didn't do it often, but looking back, I should not have done it at all. I loved him, but I wanted my freedom. I knew he was safe, and he wouldn't come down, but I guess I wasn't the best sister at those times.

Kyle did it his own way from the time he was born. It started when he was four years old. I remember one time so distinctly. He loved to visit our neighbors. He had to use the bathroom, so he went into a neighbor's home and asked them if he could use theirs. While he was there, he decided to take off his jumpsuit. After he finished, he kept it off and walked home stark naked, except for the high-top shoes he was wearing. His long curls bounced with every step without any concern, and he apparently felt that was okay to do. Now that is innocence personified!

I also remember the birth of my brother Jim when I was ten years old. Tom and I were doing the dishes when my father came into the kitchen, which was about five steps from the front room.

"Go upstairs immediately," he said.

I wasn't completely aware of what was going on. We could hear my mother crying out in pain. Tom clued me in that mom was having a baby. Immediately, I prayed that it would be a girl. Enough of brothers; it was time for a sister. My brother Kyle looked out the window in their bedroom and said, "Look, there's the stork." Kyle always had a good imagination.

We heard the arrival of Dr. Kyle Townsend. My mother had named Kyle after the doctor. He delivered all of us. We heard him telling my mother to breathe deeply. She was in pain, and we could hear how much she was suffering. I didn't like that and felt sorry for her. Then all of a sudden, her pain seemed to have abated somewhat. Maybe she felt more comfortable that the doctor was there. We then heard a baby crying. It was another boy.

My brothers were ecstatic. "Joey is here!" they exclaimed. "Joey is here!"

Joey, I thought. *That's terrible. I don't want a brother, and I don't like the name.* I wanted a sister. I was so disappointed that I decided I wouldn't have anything to do with him. That lasted until the following morning when I took one look at him and knew that I loved him. He was a darling little boy. His crib was put into my room, which was across from my parents' bedroom. I had fun watching over him and playing with him. My parents actually named him Jim. I liked that name.

Jim was born three days after the bombing of Pearl Harbor, the beginning of World War II. America changed at that moment, and I was frightened. At the time, I wondered how this had happened. I can still hear President Franklin D. Roosevelt relating the details of the attack. His strong, distinct voice came over the radio, which was the way of communicating back in 1941. He had such a commanding way about him, and I found comfort that he was the messenger. I believed his words, and he helped allay my fears. I do remember how my mother cried for the longest time. My father didn't have to go to war because of his age, and I was grateful.

I was still terrified, though, when I heard an airplane overhead at night. I would hide under the covers, frightened that it was a Japanese plane and that it would drop bombs on us. We had to cover our windows so the light wouldn't shine during the night. Men from the neighborhood wore special hats made of metal and checked the outside of the homes every night to see if our lights were visible.

It certainly made me aware that we were at war. Butter and sugar were rationed, and we used margarine instead of butter. We had to blend a package of yellow coloring so the oleo wouldn't be stark white. It wasn't very tasty, but this was wartime. We didn't complain.

One night, my parents went to visit some friends, so Tom and I decided that we would make some fudge. "Can you make fudge?" Tom asked.

"Yes, I can do that." I got the ingredients, the main one being sugar, put them in a pan, and proceeded to make us fudge. Unfortunately, I cooked it too long, and the fudge was like concrete. Tom found a heavy ax, thinking that would help us separate the fudge from the plate. He hit it with all of his strength. The plate broke, but the fudge didn't even crack. We were amazed. How could that be? Our parents arrived home shortly after, and I was in real trouble when they saw what we'd done. I had foolishly used up most of our monthly ration of sugar. I didn't forget that night for some time. I still love fudge, though.

My brothers Tom, Jack, and I went to the movies on Saturday afternoons. The cost was a dime for each of us, and we also got a candy bar. The Movietone newsreels would report what was happening in Europe. Imagine that. The daily newspaper, radio, and movie newsreels were the only sources we had to find out the status of the war. We didn't have TV or social media to keep us up to date.

The loss of lives during the war was horrific, as more than 400,000 soldiers, sailors, Marines, airmen, and military personnel perished—one death for every forty individuals in the military. Just about everyone was patriotic; we were in this together. Women worked on the line to build planes and military equipment. They were called "Rosie the Riveters." Previously, a woman's primary role was to stay home and take care of her children and husband. This was the first step in women working outside the home. Certainly, some women had previously, but they were not the norm. In fact, they were looked down upon. It was ridiculous. How times have changed. I'm happy about that.

As kids, we saved money to buy war stamps. We bought them at school, and when we had enough, we could buy a war bond. Movie stars went around the country selling them. Everyone was united for a common cause—so different from today. I remember how purposeful I felt back then that I could help support our servicepeople.

Finally, the war ended in Europe on May 8th, 1945. It was called VE Day. The deadliest conflict in human history was finally over, at least in Europe. We danced in the streets all day and night. It was glorious. Everyone was so happy and joyful, as were people all over the world. They celebrated that those fighting throughout Europe were finally coming home. I remember being a part of the celebration and was so grateful that we had some measure of peace again. The war in Japan didn't end until August 14th, 1945.

CHAPTER 4

Childhood Memories

Lift your head. Look at the beautiful clouds in the sky. They look like huge puffs of cotton. They have the freedom to change from minute to minute. You, too, have the freedom to change your clouds. They are your ideas and can change from minute to minute. Don't get stuck in one place. Be open to new ideas.

Life was so different at the time I was born. There were only a few radio stations, no TV, no computers, and no cell phones. I suppose to some people, that would seem like a distinct disadvantage, but it was actually quite nice. We weren't bombarded with twenty-four-hours-a-day news. Very few planes flew overhead. Cars weren't zooming around on the expressways. Life was quieter.

The days of summer were sweet and relaxing. Tom and I loved reading, so we would go to the library every other week and get books to read. We didn't have air conditioning, only a fan in my parents' bedroom. On really hot days, my mother would turn on the hose. We would all put on our bathing suits and run through the sprinkler on the grass with great glee. That was a huge treat.

Sometimes we picked four-leaf clovers from the grass in the front yard. My mother would weave the clover into a tiara. I was thrilled to have one on my head. I felt like a queen. How special.

We could hardly wait for the ice cream man to drive his truck through our neighborhood. We would hear his music and hope that this was the day we could buy our ice cream bars. It depended on whether my mother had the money for us to purchase them. We jumped with joy on the days that we could. The little things in life meant so much. As I write, I can remember how I felt at that time. It's a good feeling.

The winters in Michigan could be damp and cold and seemed to last forever. We spent a great deal of time putting on our snowsuits, hats, gloves, scarves, and boots, then taking them off after coming inside. Many times, after playing outside, we looked like clowns with very red noses. I was always grateful when spring arrived.

I performed in plays in grade school, and I even wrote a few so that I could be the star. I was a good student, and the nuns were kind to me. I felt love from them and drank it up like water. In the summertime, I could hardly wait for school to start in the fall. The summer was too long for me, because I missed being in school. I always wanted to go, and hated it if I were too sick to attend, which wasn't often.

We lived on the east side of Detroit until I was in third grade. My father worked two jobs, and one was selling real estate. He was successful in selling houses and saved enough money to buy a home on the west side. I was thrilled—we were moving! I could hardly wait. I would have my own room for the first time. A small bed, dresser, and tiny closet were all that would fit, but I didn't care. It was my own room. I didn't have many clothes, anyway.

I was able to choose the color for my room, and that was the icing on the cake. I chose pink. I thought it was the most beautiful room that anyone could have. It was across from my parents' bedroom. My dad made over the large attic upstairs into a wonderful bedroom for my three brothers. He put knotty pine on the walls and built closets for all of them. They loved it. We were all happy.

I remember the day we moved in like it was yesterday. I thought we were the Rockefellers. After all, we were able to have our own home, so this feeling made a great deal of sense to me. Life's perspective! That was my reality at the time.

I'm now well aware that this era was good for white people, but not for people of color. Although they had more freedom living in the North than the South, they did not really have freedom. They had to deal with prejudice, and couldn't buy homes where the white people lived. In no way did they have the same opportunities that Caucasians had. I don't get that, because we're all the same and live on the same planet. Our blood and the parts of our bodies are interchangeable… doesn't that make us the same? Color should not divide us. Progress has been made, but there's still so much more to do.

Also, we must have equality for women, although we've come a long way from the time when I was a little girl. We, as girls, were taught that our future involved getting married and having children, period. We didn't challenge it, because that's the way it was. I remember my father telling me when I wanted to do certain things: "You can't do that, because you're a girl." "Why?"

"Because you're a girl," he always answered.

I had four brothers, three younger than I was, who didn't have the limitations that I had.

Every night, I would get down on my knees at the side of my bed and ask God to take me back to heaven and make me a boy. I was so sad when I woke up and found that I hadn't changed. I was still a girl. I finally gave up and just accepted it. Of course, after my parents, particularly my father, told me that I wasn't equal enough times, I started to believe it.

I'm happy with the growth that has taken place in our society, but there's still a lot more to do. I thank all of the women who have stepped forward to try and make that change. They were courageous. Equality for everyone should be on billboards all over America—in fact, all over the world.

The Dalai Lama said, "We all have something in common. We are all born and we all die."

All people are equal, so don't judge people by:

- The color of their skin.

- The way they look.

- The amount of money they have. Having money should not be condemned. It's what we do with it that has meaning.

CHAPTER 5

My Father

One of the hardest things to do is to come to terms with our parents, and realize that they are just human beings who are doing the best they can. In some ways, life can be easier after they're gone.

My father's family arrived in America in the late 1800s from Germany, in an area called Alsace-Lorraine, situated between France and Germany. It was a territory created by the German Empire in 1871, because Germany won the Franco-Prussian War. My father's family settled in Pennsylvania and were referred to as "Pennsylvania Dutch." The family name was originally Dreisback, but some family members, including my father, changed their name to Dresbach.

Dad had two brothers: Clifford, who was like a twin to my dad, as they were the same height, was 6'1" tall with dark brown eyes. The other brother, Lorne, was 6'5" tall with blue eyes. They didn't look like they were from the same family. I believe my dad and Clifford looked like my grandfather's family. Uncle Lorne took after my grandmother's family.

Dad was a dapper man, and he was quite good-looking. Also, he was a ton of fun to be around. He was happy all the time and always woke up in a good mood, sometimes singing. He loved all types of music: jazz, big band, country, and opera. His favorite was the Grand Ole Opry. Most Saturday nights, he would tune in the show on the radio and sing along. He seemed to know the words to most of the songs.

My mother told us when we were very young that Dad worked at demanding jobs. He could work for hours, but didn't complain. After all, he had a family to take care of.

Dad was my mast in the storm, and he was the one who comforted me. I could go to him if I had a problem, and he would help. He disliked any kind of discord and faced life with a realistic viewpoint. He taught me to ride a bike, swim, play baseball, and drive a car. I got my driver's license with my dad's help. He taught me to drive with a stick shift, because that's how the cars were made at that time. It was fun to rev the engine and shift the gears. I was fifteen, a year beyond the legal age, which changed to sixteen a few years later.

Shortly after I'd gotten my license, we took a trip to visit Aunt Jean, my mother's sister, and Uncle Red, her husband, who lived in Knoxville, Tennessee. We were well on our way, driving through the mountains, when all of a sudden, my father pulled over to the side of the road. He looked at me and said:

"*You* will drive the rest of the way."

I'd driven quite a bit, but never in the mountains. I moved over to the driver's side with my heart racing. I started the car, shifted the gears, and pressed my foot onto the accelerator. We took off. I was terrified, but I was determined to do it. I was cautious, particularly when we came to a curve, but I slowly became comfortable. In fact, it only took me about twenty minutes to do so.

I thought, *I did it. I did it!* I was elated. My dad trusted that I could do it, and he was right.

My father's expertise was buffing fenders on cars. He worked for Parker Wolverine, a buffing company in Detroit. After working there for a year, the head of the company approached him and said:

"We hired you because of your good reputation, and you have proven that to be the case. We're offering you the position of head of the buffing department, and you'll get a raise in salary."

Dad was elated. He enjoyed the work, and times were good.

But after a couple of years, everything changed all of a sudden. Dad was called into the office and was told that Parker Wolverine was going to close. I don't know all the details, but it was a terrible blow to my father. He was fifty years old, had no insurance, had very little money in the bank, and he had a family to feed.

The word got out that the company was closing, and fortunately, Dad immediately had offers to go to the Middle East, Europe, and South America to work in his field of expertise, which was buffing. My mother didn't want to go, so he turned down these offers. I wished that he would have gone to any of those places, because I thought it would be an exciting adventure. One day, through the grapevine, he heard that Ford Motor Company in Monroe, Michigan, was looking for someone to be the head of their buffing department. He contacted them, he got an interview, and they offered him the position. They told him he was a young fifty-year-old, and his background was impressive. He was thrilled, as the job turned out to be exactly what he wanted.

The day that President John F. Kennedy was assassinated, my father was in a meeting, and everyone was told the news. They were all stunned. In fact, everyone in America was stunned and in a state of shock. During all the emotional turmoil, my father was told that someone was having a problem with a large steel feeding machine. He was asked to go and take care of the problem, which he did immediately.

He quickly ran to another department where the steel feeding machine was located. He saw a large, sturdy young man standing next to it, who sheepishly explained that he didn't understand how to work it. My father took over and started showing him how to run it, when all of a sudden, the tip of my dad's finger on his right hand got caught in the machine. He said he got distracted for a moment.

"Push the release button!" my dad shouted. "Push the button!"

The man panicked and froze. He couldn't do it. Dad knew that his entire body would be sucked in if he didn't pull his hand out. With great strength, he tugged on his arm and got his bloody, mangled hand out. I'm so grateful that he had the strength to do that, but his hand was torn to pieces. There was no skin left, and metal was embedded in the bone.

He was rapidly losing blood. An ambulance was called, and the EMTs quickly controlled his bleeding, sedated him, and drove him to Harper Hospital in Detroit. It was a long ride with sirens screaming.

A doctor had been called and was waiting for the ambulance to arrive. When it did, Dad was immediately wheeled into surgery. The doctor, who'd consulted with a colleague, determined that Dad's hand would be put into his stomach and connected to his veins. This was a new experiment. Their reasoning was that they could get life back into his hand, parts would grow, and he wouldn't lose it. The doctors worked on him for six hours. It was torturous for us, because we feared for his life. Finally, he came out of surgery, and the doctors considered the operation a success.

Dad had his hand in his stomach for six weeks. It was a difficult time, but because my father was who he was, he never complained. The first thing he said to me when I saw him was:

"Sis, now I'll have to learn how to do everything with my left hand."

I was so proud of him. He always looked at the positive side of life.

The day finally arrived for the doctors to remove my father's hand from his stomach. My mother, brothers, and I were at the hospital. We were very apprehensive, and we had reason to feel that way. They had to disconnect all the veins attached to his hand. We were told that the operation would be over in about five hours. The clock kept ticking. We became more nervous as time went on. It took ten hours.

At last, Dad came out of surgery. His hand was completely covered with gauze, so we didn't know what condition it was in. The doctors didn't say much about the outcome; they concentrated on the success of getting my father's hand out of his stomach. We found that he'd almost died during surgery, so it was a miracle that he hadn't.

After five days had passed, we were able to see Dad's hand. It didn't look very workable to us. Most of his palm and all of his fingers were gone; plus, part of his thumb was missing—there was no nail. Obviously, the entire operation had not been successful, but my father was upbeat and happy that he had *part* of his hand.

His attitude was remarkable. That was my dad. He always saw the glass as half-full.

We pretended to be optimistic that the operation had been a success. I thought, *He went through all of that agony, and this is the result?* A prothesis was made for his hand, which covered everything except the thumb. We were so grateful that he was alive. Ultimately, Dad learned to do everything with his left hand. It took time, but he was successful. His writing was very different, but it was legible.

My father never held it against the man who panicked. He recognized that everyone was in an emotional state the day of the accident, because of the death of President Kennedy. My father never held grudges and easily forgave. Three attorneys called him and wanted him to sue Ford Motor Company. "No!" he said. "I work for the company, and I would never sue them."

That was his mindset. He called it "loyalty." He accepted complete responsibility, and also, he would *only* drive a Ford. I loved and admired my dad so much, and I wasn't the only one.

CHAPTER 6

My Mother

The baby grows and is tended to by its loving parents. The tree grows and is tended to by Mother Nature or by human hands. The tree trunk grows larger. The baby gets bigger. The tree gains stature. It becomes majestic as it gets older. So do we, as we get older and wiser, with volumes of experience in all branches of our being—if we understand and embrace the aging process as something positive and constructive.

My mother's father's family originally crossed the ocean to Montréal from France in 1663. The king, Louis XIV, commissioned a group of young women, called the King's Daughters, to go to Montréal, because there weren't any French females residing there. He felt there was a need, because the French soldiers were there, and he wanted them to marry French ladies, not Indian ladies. He also did not send any Protestants.

The king gave each of them a dowry to leave their homeland. Our relative lived in a small village near Normandy. She probably knew that she'd never see her family again, and she had to know that her status in life would remain the same if she stayed in France. I think she was incredibly brave to go to a new country. She left everyone she knew to find a new life. Our relative got the largest dowry. We're not quite sure why, but it was speculated that she was the illegitimate daughter of someone in the royal family.

My mother's aunt, her father's sister, told my mother the history of her family. Mom was fascinated and decided to drive around Canada to get information about the King's Daughters. She went to churches, because that's where all of the records were kept. It took her an entire summer to complete her research.

She found out that some of the King's Daughters got married, and some opened businesses and never got married. Our relative married a man by the name of Broulette. They bought land, became farmers, and had four children. They were truly pioneers.

Gerry and I visited Canada one summer. First, we went to Toronto, and then on to Montréal by car. The drive was beautiful. The trees and flowers were in full bloom. We arrived in Montréal and decided that we wanted to visit the courthouse, which was situated on the top of a lovely, grassy slope that ran down to the river. We were enjoying the scenery and decided to relax on the grass and soak in the beauty.

I started to tell Gerry the story of the King's Daughters, and he was fascinated. All of a sudden, a group of about twenty people arrived near us. A narrator was telling them the history of Montréal. We heard him say:

> "The King's Daughters are responsible for the town of Montréal. They settled here. Some of them got married, and some started businesses and never walked down the aisle."

It was exciting for me to hear him talk about them. I felt rather proud. We found out that my ancestor lived on the exact property we were sitting on. She and her husband had owned extensive acreage all along the river, and they became quite prosperous.

Getting back to my mother—she was very different from my father. My dad loved all of us, but my mother definitely preferred my brothers. I talked to a cousin who was the daughter of one of my mother's sisters. She and I had the same experience. I realize now, that was what my mother had learned. Also, one of my favorite cousins, Greg, told me:

"I became a psychiatrist, because I wanted to find out why my mother acted the way she did."

His mother was the younger sister of my mother. I particularly loved my mother's sisters. They showered me with love by kissing and hugging me, but my mother didn't. I felt so wonderful when I was around them.

My mom certainly took care of me, but looking back, she seemed to be doing so out of responsibility, not love. I don't ever remember her telling me that she loved me or giving me a hug or a kiss. It was a mystery until my brother Kyle and his wife, Darlene, had a family dinner. It was ten years after my father had passed away. We had many dinners together, but this one was different. In the middle of dinner, my mother looked at me and said:

"Mary Jean, I've been jealous of you all these years."

I was stunned and couldn't answer. I thought, *I always gave you the benefit of the doubt that you didn't treat me with a mean intent, but I was wrong. You didn't give me love or protection because of jealousy.*

I tried to understand why my mother was the way she was.

She told me, "My mother was always having a baby or a

miscarriage. Because I was the eldest, it was my responsibility to help take care of my brother and sisters. I wouldn't have had all of you children if I weren't Catholic."

She had a simmering resentment that festered inside of her. Still, it was difficult for me not to resent her. If your mother doesn't love you, then why would anyone else?

Fortunately, I worked through all of my resentments and sorrow by going to a therapist. I had many sessions, and it took a long time. It's difficult to pull up old sorrows. Many times, I walked out of the therapist's office with red eyes from crying. It was very difficult coming to terms with how my mom had treated me. I realize now that she had her own issues. I can now see how difficult her life was. She was a strong, highly intelligent woman who would probably have been a successful businesswoman in another era.

My mom was born too soon. She should have been born when women had some equality or were fighting for it. She wanted equality with men. I understand that now. She graduated from high school at the top of her class. She desperately wanted to go to college, but she couldn't, because her family was so poor. Her mother took in laundry from the wealthy people in Piqua. As I mentioned, my mother delivered it after dark, because of my grandmother's pride.

After graduating from high school, my mother got a job working as a secretary in an office, but she couldn't keep the money she made. She had to give it to her mother, because she needed it for the family. My mother resented that, and I understand why she felt the way she did.

After getting married, my mom couldn't use birth control, because of her Catholic beliefs. She became very ill for the first three months when she was pregnant. I could identify with that, because that's the same problem I had. My parents were poor and were struggling to put dinner on the table.

She once told me, "When you children were young, I couldn't always pay the bills. Fortunately, the milk man and the store owners would take a small amount of money every week, so I could continue getting food." That was during the Depression, and many people were struggling to make ends meet.

My mother was lovely looking, and she wrote beautiful poetry. She had that inside of her. She studied real estate, got her license, and opened Dresbach Realty in 1948. She had two women working for her and did quite well. My mother took care of the bills and ran our house.

My mother had a colostomy in her mid-sixties because of cancer, and she had to irrigate herself for the rest of her life. What a terrible chore that had to be! She discovered when she was eighty-eight that she had lymphoma. She had one session of chemo, which made her violently ill, so she decided that she wouldn't have any more treatments. She lived until she was 90 and didn't suffer until the very end. She was valiant. All my mother's brothers and sisters died from cancer or heart attacks.

When my mother passed away in March of 1994, she left each of us more than $100,000. That was quite an accomplishment. She was very diligent about saving her money. She put it into certificates of deposit, which paid sixteen percent interest at that time.

We would say, "Mom, go and buy something that you want."

She would say, "No, I'm saving it for my children."

Mom was a complicated woman. I didn't understand her, and although she was particularly hard on me, I hold no resentment today. I can actually say that I love her. I wish our relationship had been different, but it wasn't. However, I changed my perspective as I got older. That's one of the advantages of looking at life from this vantage point.

CHAPTER 7

Summertime

One of the beauties of life is that we're never too old to change. The change doesn't have to be big; just a little idea is sufficient. We can look at our lives from a different perspective, which can bring about new beginnings.

Don't yearn for what was. Find pleasure in remembering your walk up until now. Each step brings new thoughts and desires. They may be different at this age, but they still come.

In 1948, my parents bought a small cottage outside of Detroit on Lakeville Lake. The lake was beautiful—not large, but so clear that you could see the bottom of it most of the time. It was great for swimming, which I loved doing, and fishing, which my dad loved to do. There were modest cottages sprinkled around the perimeter. We moved there for the summer, and my father commuted on the weekends.

I enjoyed wonderful days swimming in the water. I felt like a mermaid. Just a short distance down the road from us was a dock with a diving board, where most of the kids gathered. I was there almost every day, learning how to do a half-gainer from the high board. I just about had it perfected.

One day toward the end of summer, I climbed up onto the high board, took a deep breath, positioned myself, and dove into the water. The top of my head hit the water, followed by the rest of my body. It was almost a perfect dive. I was close to the bottom of the lake, which was about twenty feet deep. I flipped over until my feet hit the bottom.

I pushed myself up, when all of a sudden, something slammed onto my head. I couldn't think. I was losing consciousness. The water was swirling onto and around my head. I finally got to the surface. My head broke through the water, and I tried to get back to the dock.

In the distance, I could hear my brother Kyle screaming:

"That's my sister, that's my sister!"

That's all I remember. I became unconscious, and I was told that my brother and a couple of other boys had pulled me onto the dock. I came to almost immediately.

"What happened?" I asked.

Kyle told me, "A boy we don't know dove into the water after you did, and hit you with full force."

I was bewildered as to why anyone would do that. The boy ran away, and I never saw him again.

Kyle and his friends walked me back to our cottage. My mother immediately took me to a doctor in a small town nearby. He took X-rays and said:

"All of the ligaments in your neck are torn."

I didn't like hearing that diagnosis. The doctor contemplated putting me in a brace, but ultimately decided not to. "It will take time," he said, "but it will heal."

That very same night, it started to rain and continued to do so throughout the night. It was threatening and scary, because there were streaks of lightning in the sky, accompanied by thunderous sounds. The lightning almost seemed to strike directly over our home. We were grateful that it didn't.

Dawn arrived, the storm left, and the beautiful sun shined down, promising us a perfect Michigan summer day. We enjoyed our breakfast while looking at a clear sky. The rain had cleansed the trees and the air. I love inhaling the fragrance after a full-blown rainstorm.

Jack and Kyle decided to take out our little rowboat for a trip around the lake. It was a perfect day for that, or so it seemed. It was the weekend, so my father was at the cottage. He was in our back-yard next to the lake working on a motor with his friend, Dr. Oscar Roose, who was close to my parents. His profession was dentistry, but he'd also studied to become an electrician. My mother was in the house, and I was sunning in the yard. All was peaceful.

Jack and Kyle put our small boat into the water, started it, and they were on their way. After a short period of time, I heard my brothers arguing in the boat. Kyle got angry and jumped into the water to swim the rest of the way back. He told Jack to go back home by himself. He then decided to swim up to the cottage four doors from us, because they had pipes running into the shallow water to get bathwater. There, he could grab on to the pipes and hoist himself up out of the water. It seemed like a good decision.

Jack watched him swim when, all of a sudden, Kyle disappeared under the water and didn't come back up. Jack rowed near where Kyle had gone in and saw what had happened. "Dad!" Jack screamed. "Kyle is trapped under the pipes in the lake at the doctor's house. His arms and legs are completely wrapped around them!"

Dad dropped what he was doing and ran the short distance to where the pipes were. By now, Jack realized what the situation was. The water had electricity in it, and the pipes had pulled Kyle into them. Jack kept screaming frantically:

"Dad, don't go in the water, don't go in the water, don't go in the water. There's electricity in it!"

My father didn't hear what Jack was saying, because all he saw was that Kyle was under the pipes with his arms and legs wrapped around them. He jumped into the water to get him out and immediately became paralyzed. He knew what the problem was. His last thought was, "Isabelle is going to have a double funeral."

Dr. Roose recognized the severity of the situation, ran to get an oar, and jumped into our boat, which Jack had beached. He knew what was wrong—there was electricity in the water. He could use the wooden oar to break Kyle and Dad free. In the meantime, we found out that the storm the night before had caused a short in the electric stove in a house three doors from us. The pipes touched the stove, and they became lethal in the water.

People from nearby homes had come out to see what was going on and if they could help. Unfortunately, the people who owned the home where the electricity was coming from weren't home, and no one could break into the house to turn off the electricity.

Meanwhile, my mother was on her knees, on the sand, praying. Doc rowed the boat to where my father was and used the wooden oars to break him free. He was successful! He then pushed my father onto the shore next to where my mother was. My dad slowly came to. He was groggy for about ten minutes.

Doc immediately went back to where Kyle was trapped. Everyone had their eyes glued on the scene, watching what Doc was doing. He kept poking Kyle's arms and legs with the wooden oars until finally he got him released. Sounds of joy penetrated the air. He carried Kyle out of the water and gently put his limp body with white lips and face onto the sand and started CPR. He worked for ten minutes, but nothing seemed to work. He couldn't get him to breathe again. Finally, Doc said:

"Isabelle, I'm exhausted, and I can't do any more."

In the meantime, a doctor from Romeo, a small town nearby, arrived. Apparently, the police had called him, and he came immediately. The doctor examined Kyle and said, "Your son was unable to breathe for twenty minutes. There's no hope; I'm so sorry."

The fire department had also arrived and had turned off the electricity.

My mother turned to Oscar and begged, "Oscar, please, please, try one last time to save him, one more time."

She knelt on the sandy beach and continued to pray. Doc bent down and started CPR. After a couple of attempts, Kyle miraculously started to breathe. It was like a miracle. There was a sigh of relief from everyone who'd gathered there. People were crying and saying prayers of gratitude. The first words out of Kyle's mouth were:

"Am I in heaven? Where are the angels?"

We answered, "There are none, because you're not in heaven."

Kyle then turned his head to me and said, "I took your candy."

I had a small birthday party in June and was given a treat of delicious candy. That was very special, because we didn't get candy often. But someone took it, and I kept asking, "Who took my candy?"

Everyone denied it.

I was so moved when Kyle confessed that I said, "That's okay. I love you."

It was a miracle that he'd been saved. The doctor couldn't explain the length of time Kyle was attached to the pipes and that he'd actually survived.

"It's a miracle," my mother said.

I have no doubt that it just wasn't Kyle's time to go.

Kyle lived until the ripe age of eighty. As far as he could figure, the only adverse effect from the accident was that he lost much of the memory of his life before it occurred. He had a fabulous memory for everything that happened afterward. He was just grateful that he stayed on this planet for as long as he did. So am I.

CHAPTER 8

High School

I've found out that, for the most part, you get back what you give out. Positive thinking generates positive actions. Anger and pessimism create negative thoughts and actions. Negative thinking and negative actions beget negative thinking and negative actions. I believe in living with a positive attitude.

I graduated from Christ the King grade school in 1945. At that time, there was grade school and high school, no middle school like today. I begged my parents to let me go to Immaculata High School. It was an all-girls' high school on the campus of Marygrove College. I guaranteed them that I would go for the full four years. They finally relented.

I was thrilled, even though we had to wear uniforms. Pretty ugly! They were navy-blue pleated skirts, white shirts, navy-blue sweaters, long stockings, and shoes. I loved Immaculata and was grateful that my parents had let me go there. I was secretary of my freshman class and president of my sophomore class. I liked the girls and the nuns who taught me. I did well.

But everything changed in my junior year. I made a very foolish decision and decided to skip school every day until I would be asked to leave. At that time, it made sense to me. I liked a boy at Redford High School and wanted to go to school with him. I begged my parents to allow that. "Mary Jean," they said, "you made a commitment to go for four years. You have to fulfill that promise."

I knew that I'd agreed to those terms, but I was determined to fulfill *my* mission. So much for promises. Looking back, I do regret that.

At that time, we went to school on city buses. I decided to take the bus to downtown Detroit, which I did for four days in a row. After arriving downtown, I went to St. Aloysius Church, put my schoolbooks under the pew, and proceeded to carry out my scheme. I went to the Michigan Theater for four days and saw Nat King Cole and The Andrews Sisters, who were really great. I was elated. I saw *The Jolson Story*, which I loved, and another film that I don't remember.

I arranged to arrive at home the same time each day. On the fourth day, I was going home on the bus and saw my brother Tom seated at the back. "The school called Mom and Dad to find out what was wrong with you because you've been absent for four days," he said. "They're really mad and don't understand what you've been doing. You're in big trouble and are really going to get it when you get home."

I was terrified. I didn't know what to do. I jumped off the bus and immediately found a pay phone, as there were many on street corners at that time. I dialed our number with sweaty fingers. My heart was beating so loud that it could have jumped out of my chest.

My mother answered the phone.

"Mary Jean, get home right now," she said. "Why have you done what you did?" I didn't answer, but I knew there would be severe consequences. "If I'm going to be beaten when I get home," I said, "then I'm not coming."

I was afraid. They convinced me that would not happen, and it didn't. I went home, and we did not discuss the situation.

I went to school the following morning and told the principal what I'd done. "You have to go to school for four Saturdays in a row to make up for the days you missed," she ordered. "You will also have to make up the homework you missed."

I agreed. My punishment was that I had to clean the lockers and do whatever else they told me to do.

On the last Saturday, two girls from my grade school in the same year were also there. We'd been in Girl Scouts together. In fact, the mother of one of them was the leader. I don't know what they did to have to attend school on this Saturday, and I didn't ask. We had lunch together, and when we were finished, they asked me:

"Would you like to have a cigarette with us?"

"Sure," I answered.

It was ridiculous for us to do that, but when one is young, stupid behavior sometimes ensues.

They had matches and lit one of the cigarettes.

One of them said, "Why don't you go first?"

I took a drag and handed it to one of the girls.

Both said, "I don't think I want to smoke."

"Why not?" I asked. "You suggested it."

"We changed our minds," they said, "and we just don't want a cigarette now."

I didn't understand. I was confused. They'd given me the cigarette. Why wouldn't they take a drag? After all, it was their suggestion. We were in my homeroom, which had an opening for the incinerator in it. One just had to pull open the small door and drop inside what they wanted to get rid of. I immediately put out the cigarette and tossed it down the incinerator. I really didn't think too much of it at that time. I didn't understand it, but I didn't think there was anything sinister about their behavior.

On the following Monday, immediately after we were all seated in our classrooms, someone bellowed over the loudspeaker:

"Mary Jean Dresbach, come to the principal's office immediately."

I had no idea why I was being summoned. I got up from my seat, with all the other students looking at me, and went to Mother Loretta's office. She was physically quite short, with a sweet and kind disposition. I liked and respected her very much. After arriving in her office, she told me to sit down.

Sister Mother Loretta asked, "Mary Jean, did you smoke a cigarette last Saturday while you were here?"

I answered, "Yes, Mother, I did." I was relieved, because anyone caught smoking on the premises, outside and inside, was thrown out of school. I had accomplished what I wanted. I would now be going to public school.

"Why did you do that?" Mother Loretta asked.

"I always smoke a cigarette after my lunch on Saturday," I answered. Mother Loretta then responded: "Mary Jean, because you've been so honest, we're not going to ask you to leave."

I was flabbergasted and didn't know what to say.

She then asked me, "Do you want to know how I found out?"

"Yes," I eagerly answered.

"Charlotte and Jane left me a note telling me that you smoked in the classroom," Mother Loretta said. "I want you to know that they are not your friends. You are a leader; be a good one."

I thanked her profusely. Mother Loretta gave me one of the biggest favors in my life. I ended up loving the school and graduating with honors.

After graduating from Immaculata, I went to the University of Detroit for two years. It was a Jesuit school with its main campus about one mile from Immaculata. My desire was to be an attorney. I liked the idea of helping people. I also felt that it would be an accomplishment to be a female lawyer. After one year, I decided that I didn't want to be in that profession. I did well in my classes, which were basic first-year ones. I can't state exactly why I changed my mind, except the appeal of it had diminished.

I decided that I wanted to be a math teacher, so I changed my focus. Math had always been one of my favorite subjects, and I was put in a math class with engineers. There were five girls, including me. I did well in the class and was the only female left at the end of the semester. Again, I found out that I didn't want to pursue that profession, either.

I wanted to get a job and gain my independence. I was living at home and looked forward to getting my own apartment. But I needed a job to get the money to accomplish that. My belief is that the universe presents us with opportunities, and that was the first of many for me.

I got a position at Dodge as an assistant secretary. I liked it and it paid well. It wasn't my favorite job, but I was happy at that time. I dated and had a fun social life. I had lots of friends and a few boyfriends. And I had my own money, which was a thrill. Even though I still lived at home, because I hadn't saved enough money to get my own apartment, I felt somewhat independent. Life was good.

CHAPTER 9

A Difficult Period

A tree sprouts its leaves, sways in the breeze, and lifts its head to the sky. A tree is a tree and doesn't wonder what to do. Nature takes its course. It's more difficult for the human being. One can follow the winds of life, sway with the breeze, and lift one's head to the sky; or turn away from life, huddle down on the ground with one's head hidden, and never see the light.

Before I continue with this chapter, I have to say that it represents one of the most difficult episodes of my life. It's hard for me to put these words down on paper. I seem to want to dissociate from it, as if it's not really a part of my life. I know it is, but the memories are still raw.

After being in college for two years, my life took a huge turn. I was 19, and I felt that I was independent, which was what I wanted. I'd always been told what to do, and I relished freedom. I had a job and was supporting myself. I was still living at home, but I covered my expenses. I felt like I could do what I wanted to do and consequently made some bad decisions.

I started dating a few young men. I wasn't intensely involved with any of them, but I was having fun—at least, I thought so. I didn't listen to anyone. I started drinking too much, made mistakes, and was reckless. Little did I know the challenge I was about to face. In the late 1940s, birth control wasn't available. I woke up one morning and didn't feel well. It continued to happen, and I couldn't figure out why I felt so sick. I just didn't feel right. I was exhausted and sick to my stomach. I didn't get my period, and to my horror, I discovered that I was pregnant.

If a woman wanted an abortion, she had to go to a back-alley doctor. After much anguish, I finally decided to go to one. My girlfriend lent me the money, but the doctor said he couldn't perform the abortion, because I was too far along in my pregnancy. I was devastated. I didn't know what to do. I knew I couldn't reveal my pregnancy to anyone, because times were so different then. Getting pregnant without being married was a major *sin*. It was like wearing a patch on my arm that said I was evil. People were so judgmental then.

But I had to tell my parents. My father was heartbroken, and my mother was so angry that she wouldn't talk to me. My parents decided that the only way to handle the situation was to go to the head monsignor of our parish for his advice. I was very nervous about the meeting, but I knew that my parents were trying to help me, and I wanted to cooperate.

The monsignor treated me with kindness. "Your voice is lovely and soft," he said.

I didn't understand what that had to do with the situation, but apparently, he thought that was part of why I got pregnant. I could only conclude that he thought, *If a woman has a soft voice, she attracts men, and they have no control.* He was trying to say that I was at fault.

The monsignor suggested that I go to a Catholic charity in California. They would pay for all my medical expenses and would put the baby up for adoption. Under no circumstances could I change my mind. I agreed to it. My parents were happy with that solution and said that was what I should do. No one would know why I went to Los Angeles, so my secret would be kept. My next step was to figure out a way to get there.

I thought of my friend Pat, who also went to Immaculata. I placed a call to her. I knew I was taking a chance that she wouldn't want to have any part of going, but I felt that she was a compassionate person and liked to travel. We met, and I told her about my pregnancy. I asked her if she wanted to go to California with me. Pat immediately said yes. I was so grateful that my instincts were right. I was also grateful to her. She loved to travel and considered this an adventure.

My home life became surreal. It was like living in a place with a huge cloud of secrecy hanging above it. Except for Tom, my brothers weren't told about my pregnancy. My parents felt that it was such a disgraceful situation that no one should know. I didn't receive any sympathy, but I didn't expect it. I was functioning like a robot, instead of a feeling person.

I never told the young man involved, because I knew he wouldn't want anything to do with me or the baby. That doesn't say much for his integrity, but that's how it was. Keeping the child would make life very difficult for both the baby and me. As I said, in the late 1940s, having a child out of wedlock was like wearing a banner designating someone as a scarlet woman. I knew that the child and I would be looked down upon and that the boy or girl would have a tough struggle in life. So would I. I never told anyone for years, because I was so ashamed. I was operating out of fear and what other people would think. I later realized that this is not a good way to live.

Life can be tough. During those times, for me, it was like having a huge steel ball attached to a heavy metal chain around my neck. Taking a moment to stop could ease the pain and fatigue, but the ball still had to be pulled. That's what it was like. The hardest part was lying to everyone. I know it probably doesn't make sense today, but that's what it was like during that era.

My mother became hysterical while I was still at home. She threatened me with potentially severe actions. In fact, she said, "I will kill you."

My brother Tom said, "Get out of this house as soon as possible." He was afraid that harm would come to me.

I was moving as fast as I could. Finally, the day arrived when I was leaving. I can still see my mother's face as we were driving away from my home. It was a tragic and sad scene. She was screaming and crying. Her whole world had been turned upside down, and so had mine.

Pat and I drove a rental car from Detroit to Los Angeles. Her father arranged for us to get the car, and we were grateful. What a perfect solution. We took Route 66. I was familiar with Nat King Cole's version of the song. Pat and I sang it often on our way to Los Angeles. I looked forward to getting out of Detroit. I didn't feel well during the majority of the trip, but I kept remembering that this was the only answer. It took us five days to arrive in California.

I clearly remember one incident that happened during our trip. We were in Oklahoma, driving through the downtown area, and were stopped by two policemen. We weren't aware that we'd been speeding, but they'd clocked us.

They said, "You were breaking the speed limit. We won't give you a ticket; just have a cup of coffee with us."

Of course, we agreed to that. After talking with them for a couple of hours, they asked, "Would you like to have dinner with us?"

We said, "We have a time limit getting to L.A., and we're running a little late."

They then said, "Let us help you get out of town."

We immediately said yes.

It was close to dinnertime, and the traffic was heavy. They rode in front of us with their sirens blasting loudly. It was an exciting experience. Pat and I loved it.

We finally arrived in Los Angeles. This was the first time either of us had been to California. As we were driving along, we saw Grauman's Chinese Theatre on Hollywood Boulevard. It was a movie palace on the Hollywood Walk of Fame, and at one time was home to the Academy Awards. We stopped immediately to see it. It was a thrill for us. I forgot all my anxieties for a short time.

We got an inexpensive motel room and settled in for the night. Upon waking up in the morning, we scanned the papers and quickly found a small, reasonably priced apartment in Glendale, a town just outside of L.A. We felt very fortunate, because it was charming and it was in a good location. We didn't have TV, but we could walk up to the corner and watch it in the window of one of the stores. Also, the area was quiet and safe.

We urgently needed to get jobs. We checked out the paper and called on a couple of ads. I was very fortunate, as I immediately got a position as a secretary, working with a company that produced vitamins. I was secretary to the owner. He'd been a stuntman in the movies and had lost one leg while performing a stunt. I lied to him and told him that my husband had died. I was walking with shame. I couldn't tell him the truth.

He was a good, kind man. I will never know if he was suspicious of my story. I was just grateful to be able to go to work every day. I could fill my mind with secretary thoughts, not thoughts about being in the situation I was in. I could not become attached to the child I was carrying. It would make giving up the baby for adoption that much harder.

I'd checked in to the charity and signed every paper, giving away my rights to the child. The nuns made it clear that I could not change my mind. I was like a robot fulfilling my mission. I could not let one shred of regret penetrate my psyche.

I lived my days encased in lies. I turned off my feelings and just kept the knowledge of what I had to do in mind. I have difficulty writing this, mentioning the sex of the child, and even saying "my child." To say that burns a hole in my heart. I felt if I took off the armor I'd put around me, I'd fall apart.

Finally, the day arrived. I knew that I was in labor, but it was not yet severe. My friend Pat was working, so she couldn't drive me. I didn't want to involve anyone else, so I called a cab and was driven to the hospital. I was fortunate, as it was an easy birth. I had a little boy and was in the hospital for five days. They brought him to me every day. It was excruciatingly painful.

I just talked to him and said, "I love you. I love you. You will have a better life."

I was hopeful that the baby could hear that in some recess of his mind. I tried to separate myself from him, because I had to. I had signed the papers. It was one of the most painful times in my life. I kept thinking that now this child would have a chance that I couldn't provide.

The last day arrived. I said goodbye to my little boy and walked out the door of the hospital. It was the hardest, longest walk I've ever taken. A cab picked me up at the maternity entrance. I got into the cab and told the driver my address.

He asked, "Where is your baby?"

I answered, with tears in my eyes, "The baby died."

That was how I felt at the moment. I had to, because it was the only way I could survive. He didn't say another word, and neither did I. I tried to close my mind to any thoughts about the baby. I wasn't always successful, but I knew what I had to do. It was as though I was living a nightmare, and I was the one who'd caused it.

It is incredible to me to think about how one has the ability to do that, and I'm the one who did it. I suppose it can be called survival. In reality, the decision I made has lived with me all these years. I have to admit that the tears fall as I remember all of this. I know, though, that I made the right decision for that sweet little boy and for me.

My dad called me every Sunday. I so looked forward to those phone calls. He was my strength. I never doubted his love for me, and that helped me get through the agony. My mother had adjusted somewhat to my situation. My father told me that she was no longer angry, but we didn't have any conversations, because she didn't want to.

A week after I left the hospital, my dad called and told me that he'd be very happy if I returned to Detroit. I thought it over and agreed to do that. My family was important to me. I was longing to be with people whom I'd known for a long time. I've never regretted that decision. Pat's life had changed. She had a boyfriend and had made a new life for herself in California.

My pregnancy was never discussed again. It was as though, if we didn't talk about it, then it didn't happen. It certainly shows how it was seen as a terrible, dark secret that could never be revealed. That is so sad!

The cycle of life is different for all of us; we all have our individual paths. But that doesn't mean we should separate ourselves from one another. It only means that we can get to our destinations traveling on different roads. On the journey of life, we learn in a variety of ways—for example, listening to our parents and teachers, reading various materials, and having experiences that affect us in negative or positive ways. We can grow from all of that.

CHAPTER 10

The Starks

We meet so many individuals in our lives. Some lift us up and some bring us down. Sometimes we need to release people from our lives who don't serve our ultimate purpose. Surrounding ourselves with people who are positive, loving, uplifting, and compassionate is a gift we can give ourselves throughout our stay on this planet.

It was good to be back in Detroit. I got a job working for a food distributor, Stark and Sons. They were Jewish and had fled from Munich because of Hitler and the Nazi regime. They left without any money. Herman Stark, the father, had built a very successful business, but all of that was taken away by the Nazis.

The Starks were happy to get out of Germany just prior to the outbreak of World War II. In fact, they took the last ship leaving from Germany on its way to America. Herman took great pride in saying:

> "I was quite honored to sit with the captain for dinner every night. I knew him quite well, because my

wife and I took many cruises around the continent with him before Hitler took over Germany, expelled the Jews, and put them in concentration camps. The captain was being kind, because he knew I was leaving my country without any money, and he knew I was a proud man. I tried to retain my dignity, and he helped me do that."

I was the company's first English-speaking secretary. I loved working for them and admired them. Herman started his business in America by going to food brokers and buying crates of mushrooms, all he could afford. He then put them in his rickety old car and drove them to the grocery stores to sell them. Werner, his younger son, became part of the food business. His older son, Walter, was in the plastics business.

After living in a large, beautiful home and having a glorious life in Germany, they arrived in Michigan. Their entire life had changed. They lived in a two-bedroom walk-up apartment. Their sons, who'd been educated on the continent, worked at Ford Motor Company. They took the streetcar to and from work, instead of the bus, because it was cheaper. That was one way to save money. Herman kept a ledger. Every night, he entered the company's expenses and what money they'd made and spent that day. They had to be very frugal.

When I was interviewed for the job, both sons were sitting behind their desks. After a few minutes of telling me what the job entailed, they asked me, "Do you like mushrooms?"

I answered, "No."

Werner said, "That's our main account."

I quickly answered, "As I said, I love mushrooms."

Werner retorted, "You're hired."

One morning about three months after I started to work for them, I arrived at work, and Herman told me about a TV show that was scheduled to air that evening. It was about how the Nazis broke into homes and took the possessions of many people. He asked if I would watch it.

"Yes, definitely," was my answer.

I turned on the TV that evening and saw a horror story. Young Nazis invaded people's homes and took what they wanted. A group of vicious, stealing criminals robbed the lovely Jewish citizens of Germany. Reality hit me like a ton of bricks. I'd heard those stories, but never felt the severity of what these people had gone through.

When I arrived at the office the following morning, Herman was already there, as he was most mornings.

He asked, "Did you see the TV program?"

"Yes," I answered. "I was horrified."

He said, "I knew the young men who came to our house. Some of them had been let out of prison. I knew them as children. They started to take our possessions." He ordered the men to leave his home, and because Herman was a well-known businessman and contributed large donations to charity, they left.

Unfortunately, they eventually returned and took what they wanted because Herman was Jewish and was now looked down upon. He'd lost his prestige. My eyes were opened as to what those wonderful people suffered. The Stark family was able to come to America, but there were millions who were unable to escape. They were put in ovens or were forced to work in the camps. This is a prime example of man's inhumanity to man.

I loved Herman and his wife. They treated me like family. What wonderful, heartwarming memories I have. I got presents on Hanukkah, and one of my favorites was plum pudding. Hanukkah is a Jewish celebration that lasts for eight days. It commemorates the rededication during the second century B.C. of the second Temple in Jerusalem, where, according to legend, the Jews had risen up against their Greek-Syrian oppressors in the Maccabean Revolt.

CHAPTER 11

The Florida Years

If we only know the same things at fifty years of age that we knew at twenty-five, then we haven't progressed on this road. We shouldn't regret. We can learn. A ten-year-old knows more than a two-year-old. That equation will continue throughout our lives. Please don't have regrets—just move forward. After all, we're not going to be here forever.

We can't change the past. We can only look forward to the future. We can accept change and its directions. All of our decisions change our direction. We can choose to live our lives with either a positive or a negative attitude.

While working for Stark and Sons, I met a young man and fell in love. At least, I thought I had. His name was Richard (Dick) Tull. I'd never met anyone like him, so I was quite impressed. He was tall, good-looking, six years older than me, and incredibly smart. He told me that he'd traveled around the world and had many stories to tell about his journeys. Unfortunately, I found out later on that many of those stories weren't true. I drank it all in and believed every word he told me. *I* didn't lie, so why would I entertain the idea that I was being lied to?

We met through a mutual friend. I was having lunch with that friend one day, and Dick was in the same restaurant. He came over to the table for a moment, and we were introduced. I thought, and still do think, that it was a prearranged meeting, but my friend said it was a coincidence that Dick had come to the restaurant.

Dick called me a couple of days later to ask me out. We went to dinner, and I decided that I definitely wanted to see more of him. We went to foreign films and museums, and we started having conversations about the world. This was new to me, and I drank it up. After a few months, he asked me to marry him, and I accepted. In hindsight, I have to say that the only good that came out of that marriage were my two children, Arthur Forrest II and Valarie.

I was scheduled to fly to Florida to get married. We did that because my mother wouldn't attend our ceremony, because I wasn't getting married in the Catholic Church. I visited Dick's parents, Arthur Forrest Tull and Margaret, the day before I was to leave for Florida. His father, whom I adored, said to me:

"You don't know the man you're marrying. He's not who you think he is."

Foolishly, I didn't take his advice. Instead, I said, "Yes, I do."

It took me a while, but I found out that I should have listened to him, because I was naive at the time. I realize that we grow along the path of life, and I would not handle that situation the same way today. But then I wouldn't have had my precious children, Forrest and Valarie. I would have asked questions as to why Arthur had warned me. Of course, later on, I knew that he was looking out for my own good. I know now that we learn from our mistakes—or should. That is another benefit of being older.

Arthur was an honorable and successful man. He was the eldest of his brothers and sisters, and grew up in Kansas in a very poor family. He would walk barefoot to school in warm weather, and feet covered with cloth in colder weather. His grades were always high, so he got a scholarship to a university in Kansas and graduated at the top of his class with honors. He decided to move to Detroit after finishing college. He worked for years, accumulated some money, and decided to open a business school, which was very, very successful. He ended up opening and owning three business schools.

Arthur sat on the Roundtable of Christians and Jews, and Norman Vincent Peale dedicated a book to him. Arthur was seventy-eight when I met him, 6'3" with a full head of beautiful white hair and piercing blue eyes. He was a compelling person. He talked and you listened.

Before leaving for Florida, I had to quit my job. We lived in Miami, because the company Dick worked for relocated him there. I didn't like leaving my job, but I knew I had to. It was a sad farewell.

Dick and I started our life together, but we were struggling financially. We found a modest, second-floor apartment in Miami. Our furnishings were a small table and two chairs in the kitchen, two small chairs in the living room, and a bed and dresser in the bedroom. Florida in the summertime was incredibly hot with very high humidity, and we didn't have an air conditioner.

I became pregnant one month after we were married. I could hardly make it to work, because a horrible, gut-wrenching morning sickness set in. Also, being pregnant increased the level of heat for me. In my fifth month, I went to the hospital because I was so sick.

The doctors didn't seem to know what was happening. After being there for two days, they came into my room and said:

"We know the answer; you're pregnant."

I answered, "Yes, I know that."

They were surprised that I knew, and I was surprised that they didn't know. I was stick-thin, so no one would know that I had a baby growing inside of me. It still surprises me that they didn't know. Dick's mother and father visited us in Florida immediately after I got out of the hospital. Arthur saw my black-and-blue arms from the IVs and cried. Dick didn't even notice. His father had empathy, but Dick didn't.

It was all worth it. My son, Forrest, was born. He was so adorable and strong. The nurses carried him around, because he appeared to be looking at everyone in the hospital. They were amazed by his strength. So was I. I found happiness in being a mother.

I ignored Dick's odd behavior. He got a job selling furniture to hotels and motels, which required him to travel all over the state of Florida. When he was at home in Miami, he would stay out late at night, claiming that he'd gotten tied up with work. I finally woke up and realized that I'd experienced enough unusual behavior and decided to go back to Detroit. My dear friends Diane and Barbara helped me financially, because I didn't have enough money to get back to Michigan. I will never forget them.

I arrived in Detroit and stayed at my parents' house. I felt safe and secure. My parents loved having Forrest in their home. I was trying to decide how I could work and take care of Forrest. Two weeks later, Dick arrived at the door and begged me to return to Florida. He was very convincing, so I agreed.

I wasn't the happiest woman while living in Florida, but I thought it would be good for Forrest. Then I became pregnant with Valarie. I was thrilled that Forrest would have a little brother or sister. Before she was born, Dick's father, Arthur, called and asked Dick if he wanted to come back to Michigan and run one of his business schools in Pontiac. Things weren't going well with Dick's job in Miami, so he said yes. I was excited about getting back to Detroit, where my family and friends were.

Beautiful Valarie arrived, and I was elated. She was a perfect little girl. Forrest was intrigued by his little sister. He was the older brother by two-and-a-half years. I remember one day, I was giving a bath to Valarie, and Forrest was standing nearby with his cowboy hat on. He looked at her naked body in the tub, and said:

"She sure is a cute little thing. Too bad she doesn't have a penis."

Out of the mouths of babes.

However, my marriage wasn't moving in the right direction. Dick was going back to his old habits of staying out late and never explaining where he'd been. I tried to talk to him, but to no avail. He always had an excuse. I simply could not have conversations with him. He seemed to be distant most of the time.

I decided to see a psychiatrist, because I knew something was wrong with one of us. I wanted to be sure it wasn't me. The doctor assured me that *I* was not the problem. I was still hopeful that the marriage could be saved, as I knew that splitting up would be difficult for Forrest and Valarie. That was in the early 1960s, and divorce was not accepted, as it is today. At school, most of their classmates did not have divorced parents. But the clock was ticking away, just waiting for the end of the marriage.

My decision to leave came after Dick beat both Forrest and me. I heard Forrest crying in his bedroom, and I immediately ran to his room and witnessed Dick hitting him with force. I intervened and tried to get hold of Forrest, so that Dick would not have control of him and continue to beat him.

At that moment, Dick grabbed me and threw me on the bed and said:

"It's about time I took care of you, too."

He had my arms pinned, and there was nothing I could do. Forrest and Valarie watched him as he kept hitting me on my back. Finally, it was over, and so was the marriage. I should have called the police or told someone about that incident, but those were different times.

Soon afterward, Forrest, Valarie, and I left the "marital home," as Dick called it, and we moved to a new location for our safety. Dick had a court order to move out of the house and could only see us when it was agreed to. He broke the order the first time, then said that it wouldn't happen again. But of course, it did. It was frightening, because he would sneak into the house through the back door and hide in the basement.

One particular incident occurred that was very disturbing. One night, a friend of Dick's called and asked if he could visit. "Yes," I said, "you can come over now if you want."

The children were in bed, and I was reading a book. He arrived in about fifteen minutes and proceeded to tell me that he was concerned for my safety. "I'm worried that Dick will injure you, or worse," he said. That certainly got my attention, but I assured him that I didn't think Dick would injure me. I should have remembered how he'd hit me before.

The man stayed for about an hour, and we proceeded to have a general conversation. He was getting ready to leave when we heard a noise in the basement. Our house was built with the garage under the house, which led into the basement.

He said, "I'm going to check the basement."

I was grateful. He opened the door to the basement, which was located in the kitchen. His face turned white and said, "Dick's shoes are at the top of the stairs. He's in the basement. I'll go downstairs and talk to him."

My heart started beating rapidly. I said, "No, thank you, but I'll take care of this. You leave, and I'll ask Dick to come upstairs."

He was reluctant to leave, but I was adamant. He left with great trepidation.

Looking back, it could have been a tragic decision, but it wasn't. I called down to Dick, but he wouldn't answer. I called again, but still no answer. After the third time, I said:

"Dick, if you do not come upstairs now, I'll call the police."

At that point, he slowly climbed the stairs. "Why are you hiding downstairs?" I asked.

"I thought he was your boyfriend."

"He's your friend," I said, "who just wanted to stop by and see how I'm doing. You are never to sneak into this house."

He answered, "I will never do that again."

I knew this problem would never be solved if we stayed in the house. He'd defied the law and didn't care if he went to jail, so I had to make a new plan. I thought it over and knew that I had to leave the house, as I wasn't safe. My friend Kathy helped me with the move. In fact, her daughter found the apartment that I ended up renting on the east side of Detroit, not far from Kathy's.

I called movers and told them they had to have extra men, because this had to be a quick move. I was concerned that Dick might drive by and create a horrible scene. Kathy and her boyfriend helped me the night before by getting boxes and tagging what I was going to take. We worked until about 3:00 a.m. I didn't need a lot, because I was moving from a large, spacious house to a two-bedroom, upper flat on the east side of Detroit. It was small, but safe.

I was so nervous the following morning that my hands were shaking and my stomach was churning. My heart ached, because I had to tell Forrest and Valarie what was happening. Valarie was happy, but Forrest was devastated, because he had many friends in the neighborhood and really liked his school. I wished it could have been handled another way, but I felt that safety was our primary concern.

It was very difficult for all of us, but particularly for my darling children. After a short period of time, I took them to a therapist, but I couldn't afford many sessions, because money was very tight.

The therapist said, "They're doing very well under the circumstances."

Those words did help me, but I knew it was hard, especially for Forrest. I enrolled them in a school, and they ended up adjusting very well. My friend Kathy's two daughters went there, so that helped them assimilate. Eventually, they saw their father once a month, and then twice a month. Valarie never wanted to go with her father, but the court said that she had to abide by the order.

I believe that we all make decisions or do things throughout our lives that we regret. We can look back and say, "How stupid, why did I do that?"

That's part of living on this planet. We're always in new territory. I believe that in order to be healthy, we have to look back and say, "I know more now than I did then. I forgive myself."

CHAPTER 12

Modeling

Don't yearn for what was. Find pleasure in remembering your path up until now. Each step brings new thoughts and desires. They are only different at various ages. Wrap your memories in a silk container. Open it at any time and pull one out.

I do that. It makes me happy, and I realize that now is the important moment, never to return again. I prefer living in the now. It is tangible. I can accept its change and its direction. It's up to me. I don't have a test to take.

I was thirty-two years old, still legally married to Dick, and the mother of two children when I began modeling. I looked young for my age. We were going to a special event and, of course, I needed a new dress to wear. I went to a popular, upscale store for women nearby called Alvin's. After I'd tried on a couple of dresses, the owner came up to me and asked if I'd ever modeled. I said yes, but that wasn't completely the truth.

The year before, I'd been in a local stage production in Pontiac,

Michigan, where I walked out onto the stage as a model. I thought maybe that was sufficient and knew that I'd love walking down a runway.

Now, the store owner said, "There's a show coming up, and I'd like you to be in it."

I was thrilled beyond belief. He told me the date of the show, and I said I'd be available. By the way, the dress I'd picked out was quite beautiful, so it was a perfect day for me—a new dress and a new job.

I stopped at the drugstore on the way home and bought a *Vogue* magazine (which I ended up appearing in later on). I then proceeded to practice poses, twirls, and runway walking. I did that for hours. Finally, the big night arrived. I was full of excitement when I went to the auditorium where the show was being held. To my surprise, it was filled with 500 people. A local TV star was going to emcee the show, and there were musicians. *Wow!*

All the top models in the local area were there. I was shocked to find out that I was going to open the show dressed in a gold bathing suit under a mink coat. I found out that this was the first time that anyone had opened the show like that. I was told:

"In the middle of the length of the runway, you're to drop the coat and drag it behind you."

Alvin asked me if I was nervous.

I tried to act like a pro and said no.

I looked out at the happy crowd and saw that there were three runways connected. Two were the length of the room, and one was in the middle. All of a sudden, I was completely in the moment and at ease. I loved the music and the crowd. I was confident that I could glide along the runway. I truly wasn't nervous and just loved what I was doing. In fact, I felt at home up there, looking at the appreciative faces and their responses to me.

I exited the runway ready to make my change. Alvin came up to me; he was happy with my performance. "You're really a ham," he said. Music to my ears. My picture was in the paper the following day, and this was the beginning of a long and successful career for me. I was on my way. I still think of that time fondly. I *loved* walking on a runway. The audience's positive reaction gave me energy, and I felt like I was in a different reality.

Alvin would tell people, "I started her career." He spoke the truth.

I worked for the top designers, and one came up to me after a show featuring his clothes, and asked me to go to New York. "I can connect you with four other designers and you'll get many jobs," he said.

I couldn't say yes, because there was a clause in my separation agreement (the divorce hadn't been finalized) that I wasn't able to take my children out of the state to live. I made the only decision possible, and it was the right one. I don't look back with regret.

I did some print jobs, but preferred to be on a runway. My picture was in the papers often, some taken while I modeled in a show and some for the media. Margie Coons, who worked for *The Detroit Free Press*, called and asked me to go to New York City. She wanted me to have photos taken for what is now called *Parade* magazine. I was very excited and loved the assignment. Most of the pictures were taken at the Plaza Hotel, but some of them were also shot on Wall Street. The paper had to get permission to take pictures there. We arrived on a Sunday morning, and there were no cars driving on the street and no people walking on the sidewalks. It was so unlike

New York City.

We found the scene amazing, almost surreal. The pictures were taken on the steps of a building—I don't remember which one. I was on the second step dressed like a Russian, wearing black boots up to my knees, a white coat with a belt at my ribcage, black gloves, and a black hat that covered my neck and rested under my chin. I looked like a Cossack.

All of a sudden, we saw people following a person of importance. You could tell he was famous, because people with cameras were taking pictures of him while he was walking slowly down Wall Street. That was why there were so few people there. The person of interest came very close to us, and we saw that it was Mikhail Gorbachev, the eighth and last leader of the Soviet Union. He looked up, then looked away, and passed by us. We were all surprised that he didn't react, because I looked like a Russian. Margie and Tony Spina, a well-known photographer, reached the conclusion that if former Soviet premier Nikita Khruschev had been taking that walk, he would have come to the steps to say hello.

Spina was known as the "wandering photographer." He worked at *The Detroit Free Press* and was chief photographer until his retirement in the late 1980s. His photos are housed in the Walter P. Reuther Library on Cass Avenue in Detroit. He was one of the nicest men anyone could ever meet.

When I look at photos of myself taken during my modeling years, it's hard for me to identify with that person in the pictures. My body and mind have changed so much over the decades. The woman in the photos has an unlined face and a youthful vitality about her. I look in the mirror today, and I see lines on my face and changes in my body. It happens subtly over the years, hardly noticeable at the time, but a picture puts all that into context.

I'm grateful that I still have vitality and a zest for living. I look forward to every day, and I love the age I am now.

CHAPTER 13

The Start of a New Life

I don't want to give in to negative reactions. I want to fill my heart with joy. Sometimes it's hard to be joyful. External, unpleasant occurrences take place. It is at those moments that I have to steer my own ship. I steer the rudder toward peace, happiness, and acceptance. The waters might be choppy, but my ship is strong. I tell myself, "I can do it." It might take a bit of time, but the waters will change. I call it "smooth sailing."

I got a call one day from a model who'd been in a fashion show with me. "Hi, I'm Kathy DuRoss. Do you remember me?" "Yes."

"I have two daughters, Debi and Kim, almost the same age as Forrest and Valarie," she said. "Would you and your children like to go up north this weekend?"

"Sounds great," I answered. So, we did. We didn't have much money, but we pooled it together, and we all had a great time. We drove up into Northern Michigan, which is very beautiful. The days were warm, and at night the sky was sprinkled with stars. Forrest,

Valarie, Debi, and Kim got to know each other well and had a ton of fun together.

That was the beginning of a long friendship between both Kathy and me, as well as the kids. Kathy and I were friends until she left this planet. We both had children and were struggling financially. We lived close to one another and enjoyed each other's company. She was dating one man in particular and always included me when they went out. He didn't object. I was still going through my divorce and had no desire to meet anyone. I had enough on my plate. Kathy was there for me the entire time, always helping.

Kathy kept telling me that I should go out with someone. My answer was always, "No, no, no! I don't want to go out with anyone."

But one day, Kathy called and said, "I have a friend who'd like to take you to a Pistons game."

I immediately said, "No, I would rather not go." "Listen, a driver will pick you up, you can go to the game and then to the London Chop House, a well-known and upscale restaurant in Detroit, for dinner, and then you'll be driven home. Don't consider it a date."

Finally, I said, "Okay, I'll go." I'm so glad that I did, because that was the beginning of a new life for me.

The gentleman was fun, the game was enjoyable, and I was happy to be at the London Chop House for the first time. After arriving there, Fred Yaffe, my date, said, "Please excuse me, I have to go make a phone call."

That was before cell phones. I said okay and sat at the table, observing the patrons and the surroundings while listening to music. I was very comfortable.

As I was waiting for Fred, a man appeared at the table and said, "Fred asked me to come over and keep you company, because he's on a long-distance phone call."

I said, "That's gentlemanly of him."

The man sat down, and we talked for a few minutes. After a short conversation, he asked, "Do you want to dance?"

"Yes, I love to dance."

He then said, "By the way, my name is Mort Lieberman."

I answered with surprise, "You've got to be kidding me. I'm Tom Dresbach's sister, Mary Jean Tull."

He then said my phone number out loud. He'd been trying for weeks to get ahold of me. That was before answering machines, so I never got the call.

Tom, my oldest brother, and Kathy, my friend, told me many times that I should meet a man by the name of Mort Lieberman. They both felt we would get along great. You can imagine my surprise when he entered my life. After that evening, he called Fred to see if we were going together. Of course, Fred said no. Mort then called me, and we started our relationship. I wonder what would have happened if I hadn't gone out with Fred that night. I might never have met Mort.

Thank you, Kathy!

Also, at a later date, Fred married another dear friend of mine named Kathy—Kathy Fitzgerald. She was a Playboy bunny who ran for city council in Detroit. Fred had a successful advertising business, and he helped her with her campaign. She didn't win, but she fell in love with him. She always referred to herself as Kathy FitzYaffe. They were married for years and remained deeply in love. Fred left the planet last year. The story of their life together is truly romantic.

Mort and I went out for the first time the following Friday night to a private establishment called The Standard Club, which was located, at that time, in the Book Cadillac Hotel in downtown Detroit. We started to get to know each other and danced a lot. He was a great dancer, and I loved to dance, so the evening turned out to be delightful.

Unfortunately, a friend of my future ex was there. He called Dick and told him that I was there. The children were with him on Friday nights, and he brought them back on Saturday afternoons. I'd previously told Forrest not to let his father into our apartment, as I knew that Dick was capable of being violent. But my ex-husband insisted on coming in. I was surprised, and after looking into his eyes, I knew that I was in trouble.

He had a certain look about him when he was in a rage. He started beating me and threatened to mar my face so that no one would go out with me. He said he'd checked with the police in our district and had asked them whether they would do anything if I called them. He said that they told him they wouldn't help me, because we were still technically married. I was terrified. Also, he wanted a cabinet that belonged to me. I told him he could have it, but that didn't calm him down. He had me cornered, and there was nothing I could do. He was taller and much stronger than I was.

Forrest was frozen, seemingly unable to move.

Valarie went into the kitchen and came out with a small knife and said, "If you don't stop hitting my Mama, I'll kill you."

Dick stopped dead in his tracks and left the house. If she hadn't done that, I don't know how the situation would have ended, but I know it would not have been good.

After Dick left, I was relieved, but still shaking. I hugged my children and thanked Valarie. I tried to calm them down, but that took some time. It was frightening for them and for me. Of course, I called Mort and canceled our date. I also called the sitter. I didn't want to leave my children, and I was not in any condition to go out that evening.

First thing the following Monday morning, I called Judge Vincent Brennan, a friend of mine, and told him what had happened. We'd dated before I got married and remained good friends. "Go to the doctor immediately," he said. "Have pictures taken of your injuries, and document what happened."

After two weeks, Vince called and told me that I had a court date. I am still so grateful for how he helped me.

Dick and I went to court the following week.

The judge asked Dick, "What is your plea?"

He said, "Self-defense."

The judge then asked, "How tall are you?"

Dick answered.

The judge then asked me the same question.

I answered.

Then he asked Dick, "How much do you weigh?"

Dick answered.

The judge, again, asked me the same question. Dick was over six feet, and I am 5'7". Of course, I weighed less than Dick.

The judge looked straight into Dick's face and said, "Listen, you with the silver hair and slick tongue, if you go near her, you'll be put in jail. Do you understand, if she sees you around her at any time, you will go to jail? You need to post a $500 bond."

The judge then turned to me and said, "I'm giving you my personal phone number. If you see him or hear from him, call me immediately, and he will go to jail."

I was so relieved. I thanked the judge profusely. I finally had my freedom. Previously, Dick would tail me. I could be in a restaurant, and he would show up. I don't know how he knew where I was a great deal of the time, but it was frightening. No longer. I could now live in peace.

In the meantime, I hadn't heard from Mort. I concluded that he must have assumed that I didn't want to go out with him. I hadn't told him about the episode, because it was too upsetting for me. He'd given me four phone numbers that I could call in case I wanted to get ahold of him. He had apartments in Chicago, Dallas, and Detroit. I didn't know which number to call, but I contacted him on the second try. "Do you want to go out next weekend?" he said.

"Yes."

A new chapter began for me. Mort, who was eleven years older than I was, was an interesting man. I was impressed by his *savoir faire*. But more than that, I was impressed by his kindness, and he was also a ton of fun to be with. He exposed me to an entirely new life.

Mort had grown up in Detroit. He'd attended Northwestern University and was on their tennis team. He also loved to attend tennis tournaments. We went to Wimbledon one year when John McEnroe played Björn Borg. McEnroe won.

While Mort was at Northwestern, he also wrote for their paper, which he enjoyed very much. After the attack on Pearl Harbor and the onset of U.S. involvement in World War II, he immediately joined the Navy and was sent to Princeton to become an officer. He taught at Princeton for a while, but then was assigned to the Pacific.

Mort ran a PT boat from his ship to another destination. He never talked to me about any part of his being in the war. I found out that this was not unusual, as many soldiers didn't want to discuss their experiences.

People compared Mort to film producer Mike Todd, who was married to Elizabeth Taylor at the time. Mort loved show business and enjoyed talking on the telephone. In fact, some of his friends gave him a chocolate phone for his birthday. Keep in mind that this was the 1970s, and there weren't cell phones at that time, although Mort did get me one of the first ones that came out. It was large and cumbersome, but it gave me a lot of freedom, as I could call people from my car.

Out of the blue, another incident occurred. Mort's close friend was Bill Davidson, who owned the Detroit Pistons, as well as Guardian Industries. My ex-husband, Dick, had grown up in the same neighborhood that Mort and Bill had. One day, Dick went to Bill's office and asked to see him. Dick was ushered into his office, because Bill knew him. I don't know how the conversation started, but he did say, "If Mort doesn't stop going out with Mary Jean, I will kill him."

Mort was late that night in picking me up for our dinner date, because Bill had called and told him about Dick coming to his office. We went to the restaurant, and after a glass of wine, Mort told me about the incident. I was, needless to say, frightened and angry.

"I'll understand if you want to stop dating me," I said. "You don't need this in your life. You don't have to put up with this."

"No," he said. "I love you, and I'm not frightened."

Another incident involving Dick occurred before we got married. I was photographed and interviewed by Margie Coons in my apartment in reference to Mother's Day. I remember that she asked, "What dishes do you cook for dinner?"

Forrest answered, "We have a lot of TV dinners."

We got a chuckle out of the answer, but it wasn't completely accurate. It did happen when I had to work doing two or three shows a day, though. Margie's assistant took many photos of the three of us and put the interview on the front page.

A few months later, Margie told me that Dick had called before Father's Day and said, "Aren't you going to photograph *me* for Father's Day?" He then proceeded to tell her that the article about the three of us wasn't accurate. He said that he supported me and the children, a complete lie. This was another humiliating incident, but Margie understood completely. I didn't discuss my divorce with any of my model friends or those who hired me to model. I didn't want to constantly feed my brain with the anguish. I wanted to concentrate on my job, which I loved. Kathy and I discussed all that had happened and continued to happen. She was my anchor.

After four years of going out together, Mort and I got married at Franklin Hills Country Club in Franklin, Michigan, on August 13th, 1971. Forrest was the best man, and Valarie was my maid of honor. I had committed to converting to the Jewish religion, so we were married by a rabbi. One aspect I like about the religion is that the Jewish people concentrate on asking for forgiveness on Yom Kippur. All their sins are mercifully erased, but not the ones committed against their fellow human beings. To be forgiven, they must approach any individuals they may have wronged and ask for forgiveness.

I went to the synagogue and felt at home, but I never did join it, because I realized in time that I could not join *any* religion—I was already starting my path toward spirituality. I was concerned, because I'd made the promise to convert. I explained to Mort why I couldn't, and he completely understood. I was so relieved.

We had a beautiful wedding. Some of the members of the Detroit Symphony played music throughout the night, and we were surrounded by our friends and family. As an interesting aside, all of us models loved it when we were booked for a show at Franklin Hills. They prepared delicious lunches for us and treated us like royalty. I never imagined that I would one day be a member.

The following day, we left for our honeymoon. We flew across the ocean to Paris, then took a small plane to a town called Beaulieu-sur-Mer in the South of France. We stayed at the La Réserve de Beaulieu hotel on the French Riviera, which is located halfway between Nice and Monaco. The hotel was beautiful and enchanting and is considered a luxury establishment. We relaxed by putting on our bathing suits and sitting around the pool for a short time every day. There were quite a few women who sunbathed topless. I admired their freedom, but I wasn't ready to do that.

We saw the beautiful blue water of the Mediterranean nearby. It was so alluring, that one day we decided to rent a boat with a captain, so we could take a swim. The captain steered us out quite a distance, moored the boat, and then we jumped into the sea with abandonment. The water was soft and caressing. We swam for about an hour, got back in the boat, then headed back to land, feeling completely relaxed. It was paradise!

The French Riviera is a blissful place where palm trees sway in the warm breeze, and the sea is bluer than you've ever seen. Also, you can still spot the influences of European royalty from long ago. The region is in the southeast of France, and the French rivers stretch from Menton to Nice, Antibes, Cannes, Saint-Tropez, and Cassis. The French Riviera has visitors year-round.

We explored the entire area by driving on the three corniches, which are roads carved into the cliffs of the French Riviera. I don't think anything compares to driving on them; they're exhilarating. The hairpin turns take your breath away. You can be driving, and all of a sudden, a fast turn appears, and if you aren't careful, you can run into one of the garages belonging to the homes that sit next to the corniche, but are sprinkled high on the land. It was a challenge, but worth the drive. We also drove to the nearby towns.

We dined in Nice, which is in the heart of the French Riviera. Foodies particularly like the city, because of the exceptional cooking lessons, tastings, and food tours. One of the French Riviera's largest winter events is the Nice Carnival, a twelve-day party with floats and street events, ending with Mardi Gras on the last day. I was experiencing a whole new life, and I loved and appreciated it.

On one of the days, we drove to San Remo, Italy, which is on the Italian Riviera, because I was looking for some boots. I thought that Italy had to be the best place to buy boots. San Remo is a beautiful coastal city on the west coast of Italy. The city is covered with glorious trees and flowers. It is also peppered with palm trees and olive groves. There are mountains in the distance with multi-colored homes situated all over them. The harbor is beautiful, with many boats of all sizes moored there. The twelfth-century San Siro Cathedral has twelve bells in its tower. I didn't hear it ring, but it must be a glorious sound.

We arrived in town and looked for a place to park. We found a space where other cars had parked in an unusual fashion. We said, "What a strange way to park." We got out of our car and walked to the shopping area. There were many stores, but not all of them sold boots. The activity on the streets was energizing; people of all nationalities were strolling along. Maybe they were window shopping or actually shopping; we didn't know.

Some female merchants were standing outside their stores. They looked wonderful with their colorful makeup and sexy clothing. I was fascinated with the area. We walked until we found a store that had the exact boots I wanted. I was thrilled. We purchased them and then decided to have a late, relaxed lunch at a lovely restaurant. We were perched in front of a window, so we could continue to see the activity. After eating delicious cuisine, we took a short walk around the area.

It was a beautiful afternoon for a stroll, and we thoroughly enjoyed it. We headed back to our car, and to our surprise, our car was sitting in the middle of the street by itself, with cars speeding all around it. We were baffled. What happened? We were able to reach the car and quickly got in, ready to go.

Just then, there was a knock on the window, and there stood two policemen. We quickly rolled down the window, but unfortunately, we couldn't understand what they were saying, because they spoke very little English, and we didn't speak any Italian.

We finally understood that the parking area was only available until 3:00 p.m. The cars were to be removed at that time so the street would be available for vehicles to drive on. There were signs stating that, but we couldn't read them. We'd never heard of anything like that. It was now 3:30.

I was quite nervous, because the policemen were very angry with us, and Mort was angry with *them,* because he found them to be unreasonable. All I wanted to do was pay a fine and leave. I had visions in my head of being in a jail with dirt walls, a tiny window at the top, and water running down an old, cement wall.

I'd probably seen that in a movie at one time. My imagination was really getting the best of me.

Finally, I heard them say they wanted money. I hurriedly went into my purse and gave it to Mort. He handed it to them. "Bigga shotta… bigga shotta!" they said.

It was getting worse by the moment, and I was becoming very anxious. They finally handed some of the money back to Mort, and we were told to leave. We rolled up our windows and left the area. I was very relieved to get away.

I've been back to Italy four times, and it's one of my favorite countries. The people are friendly and warm, the food is delicious, and the scenery is breathtaking.

One evening, we went to a ball in Monaco in honor of Grace Kelly. It was truly a gala. The music, decorations, and lighting were beautiful. Jack Warner, one of the founders of Warner Brothers, was there with four models in pink wigs. I'd never seen women with pink hair before. It was unusual, but attractive in its own way.

After we left the gala, we went to Jimmy'z, which was situated on the water. We walked onto a large raft of sorts, and danced the night away. All of a sudden, the men and women who'd been with Jack Warner arrived. They danced with abandonment. It was obvious that they'd had their fill of drink by the time they arrived. After they'd been there a short time, I looked at the beach and saw two waiters put a table with four chairs at the edge of the water. In fact, two of the chairs were *in* the water. The two men and two women took their clothes off, sat down, and had some drinks. I was stunned, because I'd never seen anything like that before. It was a bright night and a full moon, so they were on display, but maybe that's what they wanted. The appeared to be having a great time. To each their own.

The next night, we went to the Casino de Monte-Carlo, a gambling and entertaining complex located in Monaco. The casino was built in 1863 by the same architect who designed the Palais Garnier opera house in Paris. It was a charming place with all kinds of interesting people gambling or just walking around, looking for a lucky table. Many women were covered in diamonds. Some were playing at the tables, and some were just watching. Mort loved to gamble, and he especially loved baccarat, which is called *chemin de fer* in France. He was successful and won enough to cover our plane fare, first-class, going there and coming back.

We had a group of friends who socialized together quite a bit. We learned to play backgammon and had our own tournaments. It was great fun. We also went to Arizona and took tennis lessons at the Don Kerbis tennis camp. We played tennis during the day and relaxed in the evening.

Danny and Suzy, close friends of ours, had a tennis court at their home in Michigan, so we played doubles. We liked being together, and it was great fun and good exercise. I ended up joining a tennis team and played on the team for five years.

Mort loved boats—probably a result of having been in the Navy. He purchased a Midnight Lace boat and named it *Darth Vader*. It was beautiful, with sleek lines, a black hull, mahogany wood, and a flying bridge. We moored it in Florida in the wintertime and Michigan in the summer.

Mort had a Darth Vader costume and sometimes greeted guests in it. They loved it, and so did he. There's a special energy being on the water. We took many boat rides with family and friends on the Intracoastal and the ocean in Florida, and on the river in Michigan.

We had parties at each other's homes and attended and supported charities of worth. We all had our responsibilities raising children and being a part of the community that we lived in. We were in the newspaper many times. There was laughter, appreciation, and an awareness of how fortunate we were to be at this stage in our lives.

Mort and I spent time in Acapulco at Las Brisas in a villa with our friends. We spent days swimming in the pool, playing backgammon, then going to dinner at lovely restaurants. We were fortunate, because everyone got along famously. We traveled to Europe together to various destinations: France, Italy, England, Germany, and more.

My friends, Suzy, Phyllis, Myra, Kathy, Bonnie, and I had a birthday club. We would order a limo and celebrate our birthdays at the London Chop House. We drank champagne, laughed, gossiped, and loved being together. These days, our lives have changed, but we're still very close. Some of these cherished friends have left this planet, but I remember them with great fondness. We were so grateful for each other during the years we spent together.

I think of my late friends with sadness, because we can't get together like we used to, but I realize that this is what life is like on this planet. I do know that there's a certain rhythm at this time of life. Kathy, Suzy, and I still get together and keep in contact over the phone. One lives in Park City, Utah; two others live in Bloomfield Hills, Michigan. It's always special when we connect. There's nothing better than old friends. Our collective history is wonderful, and the memories are delightful.

Mort and I had lots of fun, but we were responsible parents, too. I want to stress how wonderful Mort was as a stepfather to Forrest and Valarie. They called him Pop because he really was a father to them. He nurtured them and took on the responsibility of raising them. I never got child support from Dick after Mort and I got married. We didn't want it. Mort paid for their education at Cranbrook and Kingswood, a private school in Bloomfield Hills. People from all over the world attended those schools. He also paid for their college educations.

There certainly were challenges, but he handled every situation as a natural father would, and they truly loved him. He clothed them, gave them allowances, bought their cars for them, and sent them to college. They were devastated when he left this planet. I can remember my father saying, "I'm so impressed by Mort and the father he is to your kids." I was, too.

My son, Forrest, was 6'4" tall, highly intelligent, good-looking, had a great sense of humor, and was full of love. He had many friends and loved animals. I vividly remember when he was two-and-a-half years old; he looked up at me and said:

"Mommy, I love you so much, that I'd like to go back into your tummy."

I was so moved, that I had tears in my eyes. That love never left. Always, after he was grown and lived on his own, he would come into the house, pick me up with his strong arms, give me a hug, and tell me he loved me. Those moments are etched in my mind.

Forrest wrote poetry and stories, and for a short time, he wrote for a newspaper in a small town. He would go to a coffeehouse to write and read his poetry. He would also listen to the other writers reading their work. But his dream was to be a professor teaching philosophy at a small college. He majored in philosophy in college, but unfortunately, he got into the drug culture, and that goal never came to fruition.

My daughter, Valarie, was a beautiful woman inside and out. She was kind and loving. She loved people and helped individuals who were on the street by giving them food, clothing, and the acknowledgment that they're worthwhile. She lived in many different locales. She spent one summer in Japan, practicing at a dojo, which is a martial-arts training academy. She loved it and traveled around Japan. Valarie was 5'10" tall, so she attracted attention from the Japanese, who are generally smaller. It was a wonderful experience for her.

Valarie loved to travel. She lived in California for a year-and-a-half and studied acting. She was very talented, but realized that it wasn't what she wanted to pursue. She lived in Hawaii for two years and worked for an airline company. She enjoyed it for the length of time she was there, but missed her family and friends. She then decided that she wanted to reside in Michigan. She was married twice—once to her childhood sweetheart, and then to a musician for five years before he passed away.

Valarie later became a massage and craniosacral therapist. She studied under Dr. John Upledger, who pioneered and developed craniosacral therapy. Dr. John said, "Valarie is a healer. She immediately goes to the heart of the problem the individual is experiencing and takes care of it."

CHAPTER 14

Henry and Kathy

I'm aware that my life has been quite different from that of my grand-mother from Ireland. She suffered hardships that I've never experienced. I didn't have to leave my family, never to see most of them again. I am fortunate and grateful that my life took wonderful turns.

My dear friend, Kathy DuRoss, dated Henry Ford II for two years. Mort and I met Henry for the first time when we were all in the Bahamas. Kathy had asked us to go there with her to meet him. As soon as Kathy, Mort, and I arrived at the door of Henry's home, a man wrapped in a huge towel came down the stairs and said, "Hi, I'm Henry. Welcome."

At that moment, I realized how down to earth Henry Ford was. We had many fun times together, traveling or getting together at his home, or at Kathy's home in Detroit.

Kathy called me one day and said, "Henry and I are going to get married."

I was thrilled for them; they were so in love. She said that the ceremony would be out of town, without any guests. She asked me and two other friends to come to her house and bid her farewell on the day she left. We did that, and it was wonderful to see the joy she was experiencing. A short time after the wedding, they had a glorious wedding celebration in Dearborn, Michigan. There were many toasts to the two of them, and we all danced the night away.

We continued to travel together. Shortly after the wedding, we were guests at their glorious home in Turville, a village located in Buckinghamshire, England. Henry had bought the home from Prince Stanislaw Albrecht Radziwill, who was married to Jackie Onassis' sister, Lee.

Henry was a wonderful man, and we became friends. He imparted invaluable advice to me many times. And it didn't matter whether we traveled in the United States or abroad—people would see him and come up to greet him. Every time that happened, he would talk to them and enjoy having conversations with them. He had dignity, and a desire to relate to others. When he retired, he went to every Ford dealership around the world to say goodbye. It took him two years to accomplish that. I admired him, because he was caring, kind, very trustworthy, a great deal of fun, and he adored my friend. He died much too young.

One incident in our travels stands out in my memory. We went to Greece on Henry's boat and visited a couple of small islands. It was glorious to arrive in these ports and see all the whitewashed homes situated on different levels of the hills. One morning, we left the boat at 9:30 a.m. and took a bus ride up the mountain. The climb was steep, and the bus drove slowly, so it took quite a long time to get to the top.

We three couples finally arrived. We exited the bus and looked at the scenery, which was beautiful. There were small, white, painted homes situated on various levels of the mountain. We finally got to the top, and there sat a small bar, so we went in to get a cup of coffee. It was vacant, except for two elderly men with dark, craggy skin, sitting at a table playing backgammon, my favorite game. I was thrilled that I was seeing two elderly men playing the world's oldest game. They caught my attention immediately.

I walked over to them and watched them with great interest as they made their moves on the board. They didn't seem to care that I was looking over their shoulders. The speed with which they moved the checkers across the board astounded me. I hoped that I could learn some new moves by watching them. I was entranced, but they moved so fast, that I wasn't able to. Some of the opening moves were the same as the ones I used. I did feel good about that. I eventually joined the others for a cup of coffee.

We finished our coffee, took a walk around the area, and then went back to the boat. We had a glorious day on the island just relaxing and enjoying the scenery. After dinner, to our surprise, Henry had arranged for jewelers to come aboard. "I've asked them to come here with their jewelry so that you can pick out any jewels you want," he said.

I have a ring that I still treasure from that incident. Henry was a very generous man.

The following morning, we left the port for another wonderful day on the water. The sun was shining its rays upon us, and the water was calm. Who could ask for more? We were on our way to our main destination. In fact, it was the primary reason why we took this trip.

Henry had a longtime friend named Rosemary Kanzler. She was married to Jean-Pierre Marcie-Rivière. They built their home—called "Hinista"—high on a hill and called it their pleasure palace on the Peloponnese, a large peninsula in southern Greece. In the guesthouse pavilion beside their swimming pool, Jean Dumas painted the brilliant murals and windows at the top of the domed ceiling to look like stained glass.

Rosemary had a grand opening of her beautiful, new home. The date of the party was determined by when the moon would be in its full glory. We arrived in the port and were moored there the night before the gala. There were other boats near us, owned by famous people. One was Estée Lauder, and there were a couple of oil barons.

I will never forget the day of the party. The sun was shining, and there was a soft breeze in the air. We swam in the water, took a short boat ride in the dinghy, and just lounged about throughout the day. We could see all the activity taking place at Rosemary's home while we were on the boat. There were many steps going up to their home, and men were running up and down those steps all day, carrying various objects relating to the party. The final objects were the candles, which were put on each step, to be lit just before the guests were to arrive for the party.

Evening arrived. Henry had lights strewn all across his boat, and all of the others did, too. The moon was glorious. I'm a moon lover, but I don't think I've ever seen such a large, yellow, incredibly beautiful moon. Rosemary certainly knew what she was doing. We took in the beauty of it all.

We all got dressed for the festivities. I'd purchased a beautiful, full-length, rouge-colored dress in Athens, which skimmed my body perfectly. Everyone was dressed to the nines.

Finally, it was time to take our dinghy to the steps, climb them, and enter the palace. Rosemary and her young husband greeted everyone and made them feel like they were the most important people there. She was a marvelous hostess. The air was filled with a compelling fragrance, music was playing, and the most fascinating people were there.

At that time, there was a group of celebrities called the "jet set." They were featured in magazines and were followed intently because of their lifestyles. Many of them had already arrived at Rosemary's and continued to do so throughout the night. Many guests came by boat, but I remember when Stavros Niarchos, a Greek shipping magnate, arrived in his helicopter. Of course, it created a stir. In fact, for *me*, most of the people there created quite a stir! It was like being in a movie, and I'd never experienced anything like that before.

Music played throughout the evening, and I joined the other guests in dancing. I love to dance, and the music caused my feet to move with joy. I also met interesting people, ate delicious food, and thoroughly enjoyed the evening. We all did. All of a sudden, I realized that the night had flown by, and it was late.

Henry came up to me and said, "Let's leave these phonies and go back to the boat. It's time to leave."

The evening had come to an end. I'll always remember that entire night as one of the most memorable times that I've ever experienced. It was as if I were in a make-believe land, and I loved every moment of it.

The following day, we left port about 10:00 a.m. The air was still, the sun was shining, and the water was calm. Our destination was a Greek island owned by the Livanoses. Their daughter,

Tina, had wed Aristotle Onassis, the man Jackie Kennedy had also been married to. Tina and Aristotle's daughter was the Livanoses' granddaughter.

Aristotle Onassis was called Ari. He was a shipping magnate who amassed a privately owned shipping fleet and was one of the world's most famous men. He was known for his tumultuous personal life.

We arrived at our destination, and I thought we were at an island where many people lived. The entrance looked like what one might see in the Bahamas or any small island. We moored, disembarked, got into carts that were similar to golf carts, and proceeded to the Livanoses' home, which was situated on the very top of the island. It was beautiful. We met the Livanoses and then went to our rooms to change our clothes for the evening. We relaxed for a couple of hours, and then it was time to get ready for dinner.

We dressed, walked out of their home, and saw a beautifully set table overlooking the water in the distance. The waiters wore tuxedos. The beautiful, yellow moon was beginning to make its appearance. What could be more perfect! The food was delicious, and the champagne was Dom Perignon, my favorite. It was an evening etched in my memory. I can still feel the gentle breeze that touched all of us. I recognize how fortunate I am to have had that experience.

Henry told me that we would be going to brunch the next day on the ship of an oil magnate. He said that this man was having the brunch for *me*. I was stunned and didn't understand, but I looked forward to it. The following day at noon, we got into our dinghy and paddled to the ship. As we got close to it, I saw that it was immense. I was told that three men working in the kitchen had stayed up all night so that the brunch would be perfect.

We were led to the dining room, and everything was exquisite. Beautiful flowers were everywhere, and the feast was fit for a king. We all enjoyed our food and then moved to another area on the ship. I was seated next to the oil magnate, and I felt uncomfortable. While we conversed, I looked around and saw a woman whom I realized was the tycoon's wife. She was looking at me strangely, and I was so sad. I wanted to tell her that I wasn't the least bit interested in her husband. I joined in the conversation, but I wanted to jump into our dinghy and head back to our ship. I've never been so uncomfortable in my life. Finally, we left, thank goodness. We sailed away, and I did not have to see that tycoon again.

CHAPTER 15

A Beautiful Time

Memories are to be treasured. Good ones bring warmth and love into our lives. It's like looking at a picture from long ago. Each age has its own memories. I like to throw away the unpleasant ones and rejoice in the happy ones. It's wonderful to remember that we make new ones every day. We can choose to put some or all of them into our memory bank. The bank can be full of happiness. It's our choice.

I was living a new life with much gratitude. Mort brought me another special gift. His nephew, Donald Saunders, was and is a big part of my life. He's a very successful businessman with great wealth. He graduated from Brown University and is an accomplished chess player. He lives in Boston and spends the summers in Gloucester. He has many domiciles in various parts of the world.

Donald married a very special woman, Liv Ullmann. I love Liv. We made a pact and became sisters. I always wanted a sister, and now I truly have one. Liv has devoted her life to acting, directing, writing, and helping people in need, and she has been successful in all her endeavors.

Liv has won many awards. She directed *A Streetcar Named Desire*, which played in New York City and was an instant success. Ben Brantley, who was a critic for *The New York Times*, gave Liv an incredible review after seeing the play. He could be very hard on those who weren't up to par.

He wrote, "Ms. Ullmann and Ms. Blanchett have performed the play as if it had never been staged before, with the result that, as a friend of mine put it, 'You feel like you're hearing words you thought you knew pronounced correctly for the first time.'"

Liv is from Norway and has been honored by the Norwegian king. He had a huge celebration for her on her seventieth birthday, and no one deserved it more. I respect her and am happy that Donald and Liv are in my life.

Another gift arrived. In 1986, Mort arranged for my mother, Valarie, and me to go to Ireland with him. Forrest was unable to go. My mother had corresponded with a relative there for years and longed to meet her in person. Mort knew that and wanted my mom to have that pleasure before she left this planet. He also arranged for everything to be first-class. My mother had never been out of the United States, much less traveled first-class. I've never seen her so excited about anything as she was about going to Ireland.

Ireland is beautiful—the green, rolling fields are soothing to the psyche. The first night, we stayed at Dromoland Castle, Newmarket-on-Fergus. Our charming rooms, one decorated in red and one in blue, overlooked a garden of beautiful wildflowers. We had a sumptuous dinner at the Cloisters restaurant. The following morning, after having breakfast at the castle, enjoying delicious

Irish butter and cream, we headed toward our destination. We had lunch at the Craggaunowen, a 16th-century castle in County Clare, then drove to Dublin.

We arrived at the Shelbourne hotel in Dublin in the early afternoon. My mother contacted her first cousin, Jean Molhulland, with whom she had corresponded for years. Arrangements were made to meet her the following morning in Molehill, a village near Dublin. They agreed to meet on a particular road, because it was complicated to meet at the cottage where my grandmother had lived.

We arrived in Molehill and drove through vacant streets of the sweet, small town. That was Sunday, so most of the residents were probably at church. We finally found the road where we were supposed to meet Jean. The driver parked the car, and we waited on the side of the road until she arrived. We deduced that because we were on the only road in and out of Molehill, she would find us. This was before everyone had cell phones, so we couldn't make contact.

All of a sudden, a car pulled up in front of us. The door flew open, and out came Jean. She had very curly brown hair that bounced as she ran to the car. My mother quickly opened the rear door, and they embraced. It was a very emotional moment. There were tears and laughter between the two of them.

We then followed Cousin Jean to the thatched-roof cottage where my grandmother was born. I was elated. The cottage was surrounded by tall, stringy grass blowing in the breeze. There wasn't another house in sight. I found it enchanting, and I could hardly wait to enter. When we did, it was as I imagined it to be. It had dirt floors, no bathroom, and was very small. How crowded it must have been for the entire family of ten, but my grandmother never complained about how small her home was.

Two male cousins, Tom and Frank Murphy, were waiting for us at the cottage. They had my grandmother's maiden name; her mother's name was West. Her parents lived nearby in Cloone Village. Tom and Frank were delightful and looked like my brothers, Tom and Kyle. They had the same color hair, and their noses and eyes were the same. A big difference was that they were five inches shorter than my brothers.

After being at the cottage for a short time, Tom and Frank asked if Valarie and I would like a tour of the area. Valarie and I exclaimed, "Yes, what a treat that would be!"

We both promptly climbed into Frank's car. I was in the front seat, and Valarie was in the back. It was old, so we sat up quite high. They started the car, and we proceeded on. I was in the middle of both of them, and I loved it. They were friendly and warm, and they wanted us to experience going to the same places where my grandmother had gone when she was a young girl.

First, they drove us to the fields, which consisted of thirty-five acres where my grandmother had collected the peat for the fireplace. It was the only fuel that allowed them to keep warm and cook their food. We also visited the little church where she'd been baptized. What a privilege to walk over the same ground that my grandmother had! Valarie and I were thrilled to have that experience.

When we returned to my grandmother's home, Cousin Jean got a fire going in the fireplace and prepared a delicious dinner consisting of meat and potatoes. I thought, *This is where my grandmother was born and lived. She ate her meals in this room.* I knew I would remember this moment forever.

My cousin Tom, who was the local vet, lived in the house. He got his title not by going to school, but by practicing and living with the animals. Everyone paid him with a pint. He loved his pint and his job.

After we all met, my mother told Tom in a very commanding tone of voice:

"I am the oldest. I would be living here if I lived in Ireland."

There certainly was truth in that statement, and they agreed. They revered my mother and called her Granny. She could say anything, and they accepted it. She was the center of attention and adored that. What a wonderful time she was having, and so were the rest of us.

Three days before we left Dublin, Mort and I had a party at the Shelbourne, where we were staying, for all the many relatives residing in Ireland. It was fascinating to meet so many relatives; they were warm and friendly. There was an instant connection, and I felt like I'd known them forever. They all had varying careers: bar owner, actor, nurse, radio personality, and so on. Also, there was a young man who was head of a service that took care of all the celebrities who came to Dublin and performed at the Dublin Amphitheatre.

They all asked me about my "Granny," as they called her. I told them about her beautiful blue eyes, Irish accent, and how she was always in the kitchen preparing food for all of Grandma and Grandpa's guests. Their big question was, "How tall was Granny?"

I didn't quite understand why they would ask that question. I told them she was very short: 5'2" tall. They weren't surprised. Apparently, there were many varying heights in my grandma's family.

I asked them, "How tall was your grandpa?"

They answered, "Our grandpa was over six feet tall, and so was his brother. The sisters were short."

I was very surprised by that because I'd assumed that the brothers and sisters would be short like my grandmother.

The party was a success. I really didn't want it to end, because I cherished every moment. By the way, the bar bill was quite high, but after all, we were in Ireland. We didn't care how much it cost; we just wanted everyone to have a good time, and they did.

The next couple of days, we visited some of the homes of the relatives, and Valarie became quite close with one of the daughters. They had fun together and got to know each other. They were all warm and gracious people. They wanted to know all about us, and we wanted to know about them. It was wonderful that we had the opportunity to do so. We got to see their homes and where they lived. We had a very special time, but it was time to go. We had accumulated many memories, and they still linger.

CHAPTER 16

Transitions

The beautiful blue bird is sitting on a tree limb. He leaps into the air and flies with such grace. It is enchanting to watch him sweep over the trees and flowers. It is natural for him. He has enhanced the earth by being here. He is doing what he was born to do.

Hopefully we are doing what we *were born to do. Life takes turns continually. It consists of happiness, sadness, joy, sorrow, good health, illness, beauty, ugliness, serenity, confusion, being born, and taking our leave. It constantly takes turns. There are myriad lessons, if we wish to learn them.*

Mort's nephew, Bill Sable, worked for the Upledger Institute in North Palm Beach, Florida. As I mentioned, it was founded and headed by Dr. John Upledger, who'd developed craniosacral therapy.

I'd had a TMJ problem for years and subsequently suffered from terrible headaches. I didn't get relief from any other doctor I'd seen. Bill knew my situation and encouraged me to see Dr. John. I thought it was worth a try to see if he could help me with my TMJ.

I still didn't have a lot of hope, because that had left me a long time ago. Mort called Bill, and I was able to get an appointment the following week. Dr. John was booked for two years, but he fit me in. Mort and I flew to Florida and stayed at a nearby hotel.

It was one of the most profound experiences I've ever had. I was put into a room and told that Dr. John would arrive in a few minutes. The door opened, and in walked this man with a full head of beautiful snow-white hair and a kind voice. He was one of the first doctors to wear regular clothes while seeing his patients. I liked that. I found out that he was truly a free thinker. I started to tell him about my accident, where a boy had dived on top of my head. He stopped me immediately.

"Please don't say anything," he said. "I want to examine you."

He told me to lie down on the table, then he proceeded to lift my feet with his hands. Dr. John was intent on what he was doing. He then scanned me. He did that by looking with his eyes and moving his hands about twelve inches on top of my body. After his examination, he said:

"You've been hit under your jaw or on the top of your head. Your palate is completely shoved up, out of position."

Dr. John then put his soft, but most capable hands into my mouth and adjusted my palate. It wasn't painful. My jaw and head immediately felt different. I could tell that something had happened. It was a release.

At the end of the session, Dr. John said, "You don't have to wear your device anymore."

Although I felt better, I was still skeptical and concerned that the pain would come back. I'd worn a mouth guard for seven years. It was cumbersome, but it did help keep my teeth in line, because it was molded to fit my teeth and hold my mouth at a certain angle, and sometimes, for a very short period of time, I was free of pain. I drove back to our hotel and thought, *I don't know, I've had this for years. Maybe I should continue to wear it.*

Then I remembered what Dr. John had said about my jaw. No one had ever told me that before. I knew I should listen to him. I decided not to use my device that night and see what happened when I slept. I woke up free of pain. I was elated. In reality, that was the beginning of a major shift in my life. It was the start of my spiritual journey. Thank you, Dr. John.

I'd like to explain what craniosacral therapy (CST) is for those of you who haven't had any experience with it. As I said, it was pioneered and developed by osteopathic physician John E. Upledger, following extensive studies from 1975 to 1983 at Michigan State University, where he served as a clinical researcher and a professor of biomechanics.

CST is a gentle, hands-on method evaluating and enhancing the functioning of a physiological body system called the craniosacral system, comprising the membranes and cerebrospinal fluid that surround and protect the brain and spinal cord.

Using a soft touch, generally no greater than five grams, or about the weight of a nickel, practitioners release restrictions in the craniosacral system to improve the functioning of the central nervous system. By complementing the body's natural healing process, CST is increasingly used as a preventive health measure for its ability to bolster resistance to disease, and it is effective for a wide range of medical problems associated with pain and dysfunction.

We went back to Michigan and then, *Bam!*

All of a sudden, life took a different path. Mort became ill. The doctors suspected that he had prostate cancer, but they couldn't find it during their exams.

At that time, there weren't many facilities that tested for this ailment. I'd read in a paper that there were two places that were giving a special test to find prostate cancer: one was in Canada, and the other was in Upstate New York. Mort decided on the latter and chartered a private plane, because that was the easiest way to get there.

Unfortunately, Mort *was* diagnosed with prostate cancer, but he now knew he had to fight it. It was the enemy. There were different experimental options offered to us, but the results seemed bleak and unpromising, so we decided not to partake in them.

This was in the early 1980s, so the treatments were different from today. He was given chemo and radiation and fought this dreadful disease for eight years. He didn't want anyone to know about it, and that was difficult for me, but I understood why he took that stance. Back in the '80s, there was still a stigma associated with having cancer. Mort owned a business and was running it, so that also played a role in his decision.

Toward the end of Mort's life, his nephew, Donald, chartered a yacht to celebrate Liv's birthday. The cruise was to be in the

Caribbean Sea. I was opposed to going, because of the possibility of Mort becoming ill. He absolutely did not agree with me and insisted that we go and not tell Donald and Liv about his illness. I relented, but I was worried that this wouldn't turn out well.

We flew to the Caribbean and boarded the large, beautiful yacht. The other five guests were from Norway and Holland. They were a delight. We enjoyed each other, and the weather was glorious. The sea was calm, and the breeze was soft and gentle. There was hardly a ripple in the water; it was heavenly.

Donald and Liv were the perfect host and hostess. The second day we were at sea, there was a formal dinner celebrating Liv's birthday. The food was delicious, and the conversation delightful and interesting. The men wore tuxes, and the women wore evening gowns.

I was seated across from Mort when I heard the woman next to him talking about prostate cancer and how lethal it was. She was going into detail. My alarms went off. I could hardly eat my dinner after that. All I could think of was, *How is this affecting Mort?* Eventually the conversation took a different course, which relaxed me.

Immediately after dinner, Mort and I went to our cabin, because he was exhausted. I told him that I wanted to go back upstairs and visit with Liv, and I wouldn't be gone long. I climbed the stairs and motioned to Liv that I wanted to talk with her.

I said to Liv, "There's something I want and need to tell you."

We went to the stern, and I told her the entire story and my concern about the possibility of Mort becoming ill and us having to leave. She was hugging me and crying. I was doing the same. We noticed that we'd caught the attention of some of the others, but they were gracious enough not to intrude.

I said, "Mort doesn't want anyone to know, which I've honored until now, but I felt it was of great importance that you and Donald know."

She was grateful that I'd told her, and so was I. It was as though a huge burden had been lifted off me.

The following day when we were at sea, Mort became very ill. All of a sudden, he couldn't walk.

Fortunately, Liv had told Donald about Mort's illness. Donald instructed the captain to take us to port and explained to the other guests that Mort had a serious business situation and had to go back to Michigan immediately. Everyone expressed how sad they were that we had to leave. So were we.

Mort ordered a helicopter to take us to the airport. Considering the circumstances, the flight went well.

Mort immediately went to the doctor when we got home and was told that he had to go to the hospital and stay there for quite a while. He fought it and had every excuse as to why he couldn't go. The doctor was adamant. Mort finally accepted, with the condition that he have a room that I could stay in overnight.

He was in the hospital for six weeks before leaving this planet. At the beginning, I would go to a carry-out restaurant to get dinner for the two of us. I would bring it back to our room, light candles, and pretend that we were in another city or country. I would say, "Tonight we're in Paris." The next night, I would name a different country and city that we'd visited. That seemed to take his mind off what he was going through for a short time. He was valiant and strong.

I would spend the night at the hospital with him, run home in the morning to shower and change, then go back to the hospital as fast as I could. One morning, two doctors approached me just as I was about to enter his room. They told me that the time had come for me to make some decisions. "What kind?" I asked.

"Decisions about which lifesaving methods you want to use," the doctors said.

"That has been decided by my husband," I said. "He doesn't want any."

I then knew that the end was near. A nurse took me aside and said:

"You have to tell him that it's okay with you if he leaves. He's only staying because of you. His strength is unbelievable."

"I can't do that." I felt like I was handing him a death sentence.

I called Dr. John to see if he could come and help Mort. He flew in, examined him, and said, "The disease has taken over; when that happens, there's nothing that can be done."

I was grateful that he saw Mort, but devastated with his prognosis.

Valarie and I sat by his bed for two days. Forrest came in at intervals.

Finally, after much thought, I realized that I was prolonging my husband's suffering, as I could see what he was going through. I didn't want him to suffer anymore. It was one of the hardest decisions that I'd ever made, but I told him:

"You are so valiant and strong. I understand if you want to leave. I don't want you to suffer anymore."

I also said gently and with love, "Your parents and sisters are on the other side. They love you very much, and you love them."

He listened intently and went into a coma shortly after that. I held him in my arms and said goodbye. Mort passed away the following day.

The most amazing event took place as he was leaving. After his last breath, Valarie and I saw the skin on his entire body light up, and then light spiraled up out of the middle of his head. We were speechless. We just looked at each other, not knowing what to think. Since then, other people have told us that they've had the same experience when their loved ones left.

Popular Detroit disk jockey and interviewer J.P. McCarthy announced on the air, "I just found out that one of the nicest men I've ever known, Mort Lieberman, passed away. He will be missed greatly."

I had a grand funeral for Mort. I wanted to honor him, because he deserved it. He was a kind soul who helped many people while he was here. For example, he sent four young men to college, giving donations to various charities and to individual families who had very difficult lives financially.

Among the many charities that he supported was his favorite, the Thanksgiving Parade in November in downtown Detroit. He had a clown outfit that he wore in the parade. He also sponsored a Detroit marching band comprised of young Black students. He got so much pleasure doing things like that.

CHAPTER 17

Changing Perspectives

Each age has its own trials and tribulations. Some are smaller, and some are larger. At this age, I believe that I'm able to sort out their relative importance. I also believe that it's important to acknowledge the benefits of whatever age we are right now. That's one thing I wish I'd known when I was young. But maybe we're supposed to find that out toward the end of life.

Life can take many turns. One may not realize at the time when something happens, that it's a fortunate occurrence. The future is unseen, and I believe that we need to take chances. I don't want to live in a safe cocoon. I want to continue to grow and live life to the fullest. I can truthfully say that this is what I'm doing now. In some strange way, this age inspires me more than any other to live in this way. I am so grateful to be this age.

Life certainly altered considerably for me when Mort passed. I mourned for a year, as I wanted to honor Mort in light of his long, difficult illness. After that period of time, a friend visited me and said that I should get on with my life. Easier said than done, but I knew she spoke the truth.

We're never too old to look at life from a different perspective. That's the beauty of our existence. It is constantly changing. The changes don't have to be big; just a small idea is sufficient. Curiosity didn't kill the cat—it brought about new beginnings. It all depends on how we choose to live.

I knew that I wanted to have a new life, even if it was very different from how I'd been living. It's true that during my years with Mort, I'd lived a life of privilege—the best tables at the best restaurants, traveling to New York to shop for clothes at all the high-end stores, flying to Europe many times and to events around America.

One example was attending the 1973 Bobby Riggs/Billie Jean King tennis match in the Houston Astrodome with our friends Danny and Suzy. The stadium was filled to capacity and marked the highest attendance ever for a tennis match: 30,492 fans came to see this "Battle of the Sexes." There was a feeling of excitement in the air, and the purse was winner-takes-all. It was a thrill for me, because I played on a tennis team in Birmingham, Michigan at that time.

Bobby Riggs had been the number-one tennis player in the world for three years, and he was convinced that he would win, as did many others. At the time, Bobby Riggs was fifty-five, and Billie Jean King was twenty-nine. Billie Jean was a fabulous tennis player as well, and she proved it by winning the match, as well as the cash award of $100,000. The match was dubbed the "Mother's Day Massacre."

About two months later, Riggs was in town for a charity event, which Mort and I attended. Many of our friends were there. Riggs claimed to be an expert at backgammon, and any person who played him and lost would have to donate $50. He announced, "I can beat everyone!"

Well… I approached him and told him I'd like to challenge him to a game. He got a big smile on his face and was ready to knock me out of the box. I sat down across from him, and the game started. The dice were being kind to me, my moves worked, and I won. He couldn't believe that I'd beaten him, so he challenged me again. I really didn't want to, but I knew I had to. I did, and I won again. He was very disappointed and didn't challenge me again, which I was happy about.

However, my outlook regarding the way I wanted to live my life was changing. The thrill of constantly being in the paper after charity balls that we attended and always having the best seats when we went to any event was waning. And being a member of three different country clubs didn't excite me, either. I found that I was going in a different direction. All the hoopla had lost its allure.

I've met people from all walks of life. Some are immensely wealthy, living lives without any financial worries. Some are struggling to make it to their next paychecks. And some are in the middle, living lives where they're not desperate, but where they have to be careful about how they spend their money. People may think that because others have wealth, their lives are trouble-free. That is simply not true. We all experience hardships. What's important is how we handle them.

I've been privileged to have met the people I have. They are as different as various candies in a jar. Their paths have been different, as have their likes and dislikes, goals for happiness, and levels of notoriety. However, each individual has been special to me. Some of our beliefs have been at opposite ends of the social and political spectrum, but there's always been a thread that connects us.

One day, some members of our golf club called and asked me to go out with them. They were nice individuals, but I wanted a change. I didn't know it at the time, but I was on a search for spirituality. I knew in my heart that it was time for me to find peace.

I eventually bought a townhouse in Florida. I was familiar with the area, because Mort and I had vacationed in the West Palm Beach area. I had my eye on one place in particular. When we drove by, I'd say, "I'd love for us to have one of those townhouses."

Mort would answer, "Put a note on the door of one, and tell them that you're interested in buying one."

I never did—primarily because there was never one for sale.

Four months after Mort passed, Valarie was in Florida attending a conference at the Hilton Hotel in Jupiter. She was a massage therapist and was furthering her knowledge by taking lessons in craniosacral therapy from Dr. John Upledger. She decided to drive by the townhouses that I'd always admired. Surprisingly, one was for sale. She was so excited and called me immediately, exclaiming, "Mom, there's a townhouse for sale!"

I could hardly believe my ears. I asked her to get the contact phone number, which she'd already done.

I called the real estate agent and asked the price. I found it to be reasonable and arranged for Valarie to go through it and then give me her opinion. She loved it. I made an appointment to fly to Florida to see it for myself. From the way she described it, I was quite sure that I'd buy it. And I was right.

It was the beginning of a new life for me. Within four months, I moved for the winter to my new townhouse. I had moments where I asked myself, "What have I done?" I was frightened and in new territory. But ultimately, it turned out to be a good decision. It was a beginning of a new life that I wanted to live for the rest of my years. It is one of the best things I've ever done.

I started donating my time to the Brain and Spinal Cord Program at the Upledger Institute. I took videos while Dr. John performed miracles on his patients. (They gave their consent ahead of time.)

I remember one case in particular. A young college student was attending a university up north. He was in his third year, when there was a sudden snowstorm. Six inches fell to the ground overnight while he was sleeping. He got up in the morning, looked out his window, and saw heaps of snow on the ground. He dressed and hurried off to his classes. While attempting to cross the street to get to his class, he slipped while stepping off the edge of the curb and fell with force. He hit his head on the cement and couldn't move. Another student saw what had happened and immediately called an ambulance, which arrived within minutes. The young man was taken to the hospital, where he was told he was now a quadriplegic. His life had changed forever.

After a certain period of time, his family heard about the Upledger Clinic. They felt that it was their only hope. The young man applied and was accepted. As he was being treated by Dr. John and three assistants, I was taking a video, standing about three feet in front of his body. All of a sudden, I was hit by a gust of air that almost made me lose my balance. I didn't know what hit me.

Dr. John said, "I guess you're wondering what just happened."

I answered, "Yes!"

He said, "That is energy that came from his body. There is energy there, even though he can't move."

Dr. John was able to help this young man. Although he wasn't able to regain all of his movement, there was progress. That was my first experience dealing with energy. I didn't know it then, but my spiritual journey was taking a new turn.

CHAPTER 18

Love Arrives

Every day we make new memories. We can make happy ones or unhappy ones. Some we don't have any control over: illness, death, unfulfilled relationships, new friends, and loving old friends. Life is constantly moving. Each day is different.

Some days, we get up ready to face the world. Some days everything seems more difficult. The flow changes. We can change from hour to hour. However, we can influence it somewhat by our attitude. We can be accepting, understanding, and positive. Or we can want to have everything our way and fight the natural flow of life. It's so much easier to let go and relax. Everything works out so much better that way.

I have a friend named Jutte who was born in Germany. She married a well-known photographer and artist, Charlie Schridde, and lived in the United States for twenty years. Jutte is 5'10" tall, good-looking, and very talented. She had two children and became a citizen of the United States. We modeled together, became friends, and had lunch a couple times a year after we retired. We met for lunch one day in 1980. I suggested going to Franklin Hills Country Club, because that was one of Jutte's favorite places. She was thrilled.

During lunch, we caught up on what we'd each been up to since our last meeting.

Jutte said, "I've been thinking of remodeling houses and then selling them."

Surprised, I said, "I've been thinking about the same thing."
"I'm serious," she said.

"So am I."

She then pulled a piece of newspaper from her purse that had houses for sale, to show me how seriously she'd been about buying one. We perused the paper and immediately decided to form a business. Now we had to look for a house to flip.

We formed our business and got cards printed with our names on them. We were excited to be businesswomen. We spent just a few days looking for a house before we found one in Birmingham, Michigan. We knew that it was the one we wanted as soon as we walked in the door. The bones of the house were solid: beautiful wooden floors, a great yard, and a good location.

We made an offer, and it was accepted. Finally, all the paperwork was attended to, and the day had arrived for us to close. We went to the real estate office with our mink coats on, carrying attaché cases. After all, we were now professionals. We had a bottle of champagne in my car to celebrate the closing on this very important day.

We closed the deal and went to the house to have that glass of champagne. We were standing in the living room looking around, feeling very proud and excited. We both looked up at the false ceiling at the same time.

I said, "Instead of drinking our champagne, let's take the ceiling down."

Jutte agreed immediately; she thought it was a good idea.

We both shed our coats and went right to work. It was wonderful.

We were there every day from 9:00 a.m. until 5:30 p.m. and loved it. We found out that we agreed on almost everything, and fortunately, we had the same taste. We did as much work as we could and only had contractors in when we didn't know how to do what needed to be done. I papered the walls of a bedroom, which I'd never done before, and it turned out great. It was a new experience, and I really enjoyed the work. One day, some friends stopped by and just shook their heads, wondering why we'd bought the place. They didn't have the vision that we did. We knew that the bones of the house were excellent. They came back after the renovations were complete, and were surprised and thrilled with the finished product.

We loved doing this type of work and were very successful when we sold this home. We decided to buy another house to remodel, and that turned out to be fruitful as well. We were successful businesswomen and proud of it. We worked almost every day and thoroughly enjoyed our new endeavor, but we only worked on those two houses. Times changed. I bought out Jutte's stake in the house, rented it for five years, then sold it.

I was delighted, because one year after I'd moved to Florida, Jutte and her husband came to visit and loved my townhouse so much, that they decided they wanted to buy one, too. Fortunately, one was available two doors over. Jutte's husband traveled quite often, because he was a sought-after photographer. Charlie did a great deal of work for the auto companies, and the shoots were in different parts of the country. Jutte and I ended up spending a lot of fun times together. Life was good.

She kept telling me that she had a male friend I should meet, because she thought we had a lot in common.

I told her, "I'm not interested in meeting anyone. I have no intention of dating or ever getting married again. I'm going to devote my life to works of charity." I was still donating my time to the Upledger Institute, and I loved it.

So much for that theory. The man Jutte had talked about visited her home in October of 1989, when I was fifty-eight years old. His two sons, Robert and Jonathan, had arrived two days earlier. They were friends with Jutte's children. She asked me over for dinner and introduced me to this man, whose name was Gerry Teachman. He was fifty-one. I was impressed by him. He exuded kindness, and I was surprised that we had so many things in common.

Coincidentally, we'd both spent time in Piqua, Ohio when we were young. Previously, when I'd mention Piqua to anyone, they'd never heard of that town and didn't have any idea where it was located. You can imagine my surprise when Gerry said, "Yes, I visited friends of my family there a few times."

Also, both of our fathers were named George. Gerry's name is actually Gerard, which was my mother's maiden name. I certainly was intrigued by all of that. Also, his beautiful, soft, kind, and brilliant blue eyes caught my attention.

Jutte was a gourmet cook and prepared a fabulous dinner, which we thoroughly enjoyed. We also sipped delicious wine and laughed together. The evening flew by. I was surprised by how much I truly enjoyed myself.

Gerry walked me two doors down to my home. We went onto the porch and marveled at how beautiful the moon was shining down on the ocean. It was truly magical. I *did* feel a connection, but I didn't want to get involved. I still wanted to honor Mort for a while longer, because he'd been sick for eight years. He'd fought like a trooper all that time, and I didn't feel like dating was the right thing for me to do yet. I've never regretted that decision. We lingered for a few minutes, then Gerry went back to Jutte's.

The following day, Gerry, Jutte, and I went to the beach in front of my house. The day was glorious. The sun shined gently down on us, and the sand on the beach glistened. I could see in the broad daylight how handsome Gerry was. While playing gin rummy with him, I also found out that he had a great sense of humor. I did pretty well that day by winning most of the games. He claims that he *didn't* just let me win. I believed him, because honesty flows out of him like a faucet.

Gerry's two sons, Robert (the older son) and Jonathan, were there, too. Robert was (and is) bright, fun to be with, good-looking, a great cook, and very smart. He'd been a very successful photographer for years, working on car commercials. All of a sudden, the industry changed drastically and stopped using photographers. He had to find a new position, which he did. He now works for Apple and loves it. He was single, but had been married and divorced before I met him. We immediately got along.

Jonathan is a little person, and a very special individual. Of course, I didn't know that at the time, but I could sense it. I saw Gerry's interaction with him and got teary-eyed, because of the wonderful relationship they had. I could see that Gerry was a great father to both of his sons, and that impressed me.

It isn't easy being a little person. Jonathan has challenges that many other people don't have. He never complains and is always grateful. People take to him immediately, because his sense of humor is similar to that of a comedian. While he was in college, he was hired to be the opening act at the Comedy Club in Birmingham, Michigan. Two days before the opening, he was hit by a car while riding his bike near his home. He was in a coma for two weeks and had to have therapy for months. Thankfully, he recovered. He's now married to Carolyn, who is also a little person. They live a very happy life.

Three days a week, Jonathan devotes his time to an Alzheimer's day-care center. The men particularly love him. They don't like the women very much, because they associate the female helpers with their wives. Usually, their wives take them there for the day, and that can make them angry. Jonathan is like a grandson to them, and they don't hold him accountable for them being where they don't want to be. Of course, the women caregivers care for them as well.

Jonathan plays original music on a keyboard and plays cards with these men. He's always finding new ways to reach out to them. One year, he won an award for being a volunteer. The prize was presented to him at a luncheon at Greenfield Village in Dearborn, Michigan.

Back to being at the beach. We spent a lovely day there. Gerry left that day, because he had a commitment to visit a friend of his. I knew that I was attracted to him, but I still felt that it was too soon after Mort had passed to get involved. Gerry called me after he arrived home and said, "When you come to town, if you want to have dinner, please call me." I told him that I would.

I went back to Michigan in the spring of 1990 to sell my house, and my brother Kyle wanted to have a party for me. I thought that was a wonderful idea, and I asked Jutte to come.

"I'd love to go," she said. "Are you going to ask Gerry?"

"Yes," I answered.

A couple of days went by, and Jutte asked, "Have you called Gerry?"

"No."

She offered to call for me. "No, I'll do it." I was a little nervous to take that step, but a few days later, I called Gerry and asked him if he'd like to go to a party with me.

He said yes and asked, "What time should I pick you up?"

I don't know why, but I answered, "7:06."

He didn't understand why I'd picked that time, and neither did I. It was a whimsical answer. He went along with it and picked me up at that exact time. I was impressed. That was the first of many occurrences between us that made a good impression on me.

The party was terrific; it was a gala. Kyle knew how to make a party a ton of fun. My family and friends, many of whom I hadn't seen in months, were there. Oh, the joys of friendship! Shortly after I got there, my brother Jack came up to me and said, "I won't tell him your age."

I was taken aback. I said, "I'm seven years older than Gerry, and he knows that. What difference would that make?" I rather like the fact that I'm older than he is. Age is only a number.

An interesting event occurred at that party. I realized that I was territorial when it came to Gerry. I'd never been that way with any other man before. He knew some of the people who were there and was having a good time connecting with them, but I thought he should have been spending his time with me. I knew that was ridiculous, because I was also socializing with many of the guests who'd come to the party. I realized that I was having a new experience, and I enjoyed it. It was the beginning of a relationship that I'd never experienced before.

Gerry and I clicked immediately. I respected him for his devotion to teaching. He had a multifaceted career teaching high school students in the inner city and the wealthy suburbs. He was also a professor of philosophy at Wayne State University, where he'd gotten his PhD. And he was an education consultant for the State of Michigan, assigned as staff to the federal court desegregation of the Detroit Public Schools. He stayed there for twelve years. He's now retired, but he is still devoted to education and what is happening in the inner city schools. He wrote a book, *Tales Out of School*, which has been well received.

Another reason I respect and love Gerry so much is because of his close friendship with Jean Peters, who was born in 1921 in Alabama and died in 1996 in Detroit at the age of seventy-five. Jean was Black. His father was light-skinned and had a PhD in history from Tuskegee University. His mother, who was brown-skinned, also graduated from a Black university with a degree in engineering. They both ended up being teachers in a small town in Alabama, where they raised two sons and a daughter.

Jean, the oldest son, who was named after Jean Valjean, from Victor Hugo's classic book, *Les Misérables*, had tried in vain to have people pronounce his name as the French would. He received three degrees, including a PhD in educational leadership. His younger brother had a Doctor of Divinity degree, and his sister had a Master's degree in nursing. I never met his sister, but I did meet his brother. There was a party for Jean, and his brother was the emcee. He had a terrific sense of humor; I found him to be witty, funny, and an individual with great integrity. The crowd enjoyed his repartee, and so did I.

After receiving his BA at Tuskegee in 1942, Jean enlisted in the U.S. Army. He wanted to be a pilot, but his eyesight wasn't good enough. Jean was about 5'10" tall, with an athletic build, curly hair, and light-brown skin. He became an infantry lieutenant, graduating from Officer's Candidate School at Tuskegee, and ended up a captain. He fought in Europe in an all-Black battalion and received a Bronze Star. He was released from the Army in 1946 and was called back in 1950, at the start of the Korean War. He was promoted to major, and was in a newly-integrated battalion in Korea, where he earned another Bronze Star.

Jean told us that the most frightening thing he ever experienced took place in his hometown in Alabama. He was a captain who'd just arrived home after World War II. He was walking down the main street of the town in his uniform when three white enlisted men walked toward him, looked straight at him, and didn't salute. Jean stepped in front of them, forcing them to stop, and said, "I don't care what you think of me, but I'm a U.S. Army officer, and you are U.S. Army enlisted men. You will not disrespect the uniform I wear so proudly."

The men saluted him. Jean went into a store, and when he came out, there must have been at least forty white men waiting for him. Jean had heard all the stories about what white southern men in Alabama did to "uppity" Black men, but he felt empowered by his uniform. He walked straight toward the group, and after a tense moment, they parted to let him through. Jean said, "I was shaking the whole time."

He went back to Atlanta in 1954, after having defended his country in two wars, the other one being the Korean War, and found out that he still couldn't vote. He became a community organizer in his county, and eventually won the right to vote for a group of local farmers.

Jean married and had two children, a girl and a boy. Jean moved his family to Detroit, because of the Jim Crow laws. He became a schoolteacher in the Detroit public school system, and then Jean's wife suffered what was then called a nervous breakdown. After many years of unsuccessful treatment, she eventually went to an institution for the rest of her life.

Jean spent his entire life working in education and with young people through his church. He died from cancer in 1996. After all the injustices he suffered, Jean always remained a polite, proud man, a dedicated educator, and a true friend to Gerry, and then me. He even left his sickbed to come to Forrest's memorial service (I'll explain more about this in the next chapter). I hugged him and thanked him. He smiled and said, "That's what friends are for."

I cherished his friendship.

Gerry's life journey has been influenced by philosophy. Mine has been spirituality. I believe in reincarnation and that we're here to learn lessons. Our different approaches to life work very well together. I know that we were meant to meet in this lifetime, and he has encouraged me every step of the way in my quest to find peace of mind.

We got married on September 20th, 1991, and it was a lovely wedding. We were surrounded by family and a few friends. A woman who played the harp sent beautiful music throughout our home. The September weather had a soft breeze to it, and some people had gathered around the pool to enjoy the glorious setting of the sun.

We were married in our living room in front of the fireplace. An old friend of Gerry's, Judge Michael Connor, married us. Forrest, Valarie, Robert, and Jonathan were our best men and woman. It was lovely as we exchanged our vows. A new life was beginning for all of us. Jutte told everyone that she was responsible for this, because she'd introduced us. And she was right.

We had a glorious honeymoon on the island of Anguilla. We stayed at the Cap Juluca Resort located on a mile of white sand along Maundays Bay. Our villa was situated on the sand, close to the clear, blue water. Every morning, our breakfast was brought to us by two women who put it on the table outside on our veranda. After we'd finished our breakfast, we were visited by sweet, little birds who sat on our table and helped themselves to breakfast. They were our little visitors. There was peacefulness all around us.

We took long walks on the pristine sand beaches and explored all the different parts of the island. Anguilla is known as both the northernmost and best Caribbean Island. St. Martin is the closest by twelve miles. One of the surprising things we learned is that quite a few of the natives had never left the island. When we asked them why they hadn't traveled to the nearby island, which was only ten minutes by boat, they said, "Why? It's so beautiful here."

And they're right. It *is* beautiful. Some say that Columbus sighted the island in 1493 on his second voyage to the West Indies. After ten days of being carefree and incredibly relaxed, we returned to our life in Michigan.

Gerry continued teaching at the high school in Birmingham, as well as at Wayne State University. Living with him made me realize what a good teacher he was. He put in a great deal of time preparing. He listened to his students and called them by "Ms." or "Mr." and their last names, as a sign of respect. They addressed him as Dr. Teachman. He had students who lined up to get into his classes, and his impact was felt by many. I developed a whole new level of respect for teachers and realized how dedicated most of them are.

We traveled to the Orient, France, Italy, Germany, Vienna, and Norway. We have many memories, but one trip in particular is etched in my mind. We rented a lovely villa in Tuscany with my brother, Tom, and his wife, Jan. The atmosphere was serene, with horses grazing on the hillside, as we enjoyed incredibly delicious food with the breezy air surrounding us.

We traveled by car to Pisa and saw the leaning tower. We drove through rolling hills full of cypress trees and lovely vineyards. We laughed, ate mouthwatering food, and drank delicious Italian wine. The Italian people were very friendly, and we were incredibly happy. I can still hear the laughter that we shared every day.

We then went to the Amalfi Coast, which is breathtakingly lovely. We stayed at the San Pietro di Positano hotel on the top of a mountain. Upon waking every morning, we would go onto our private terrace with its sea view and look down below at the olive trees and green grass. We would see three or four Italian women wearing long dresses with white aprons. They would heartily shake an olive tree, then place the olives that fell to the ground in their large pockets. I carry that image with me, and I take joy in remembering it.

We visited Donald and Liv many times in Norway during the

summers, and each visit was special. Liv has a home in Sandefjord, which is located in western Norway, and she also has an apartment in Oslo. Her home in Sandefjord is on the fjord. It is beautiful and exudes great warmth and joy. We walked the scenic, serene country-side and swam in the fjord. I have to admit that I just did it once, because it was so cold. We met Donald and Liv's many wonderful friends, whose hospitality made it feel as if we'd known them for years. One year, the Tall Ships were in the harbor, and we spent the evening on one of them, drinking beer and eating small shrimp.

Norway is known as the "land of the midnight sun." There are seasonal variations in daylight, because the period of refracted sunlight is long. The sun never sets for twenty hours for about sev-enty-six days, from late May to late July. I found the nights to be magical. I loved looking up at the sky at eleven o'clock at night and seeing what looked like a little sunlight with many stars sprinkled above us. Being on the fjord surrounded by the sea and lush vegeta-tion is etched in my memory, and it flows through my veins, creat-ing happiness.

CHAPTER 19

Tragedy Strikes

Living presents challenges to all of us. No one is exempt. We may look at our fellow men and women and think that some of them live "perfect" lives, but the reality is that we all have issues to resolve, every day. We take care of one issue, and another arrives. Life is always in flux.

I believe that life is what we make it. There are extenuating circumstances that cause hardships, loss, anger, sickness, and anxiety. I know that my role is to accept it and go on. It will never be the same, but I can find joy, love, and happiness by accepting what is.

Gerry and I merged our families, and life was good. We were grateful that we'd found each other at this time of life, and we were very much in love. In fact, I'd never had a relationship like ours. Then tragedy struck. My beloved son, Arthur Forrest, at the age of thirty-eight, took his life with a gun. He'd struggled for years with bipolar disease, and he'd self-medicated through drugs and had become addicted to heroin. It's not unusual for people with a brain disease to latch onto drugs. Drugs make them feel better.

However, Forrest had kicked his drug habit and had been clean for the past four years. He was taking methadone to help him get over his addiction. He went once a week to the clinic to get his dose, and at one of the sessions, a man who was working at the facility giving out the methadone approached him and asked, "Why are you doing what you're doing?"

Forrest answered, "Because I can't stop."

The man responded, "I know how you can stop."

Forrest didn't believe that and left without asking him how.

Forrest thought about that question for a week and decided that he'd ask the man how he could break his terrible habit. He arrived at the methadone clinic, went to the gentleman, and asked him, "How can I stop?"

"Go to my church on Sunday," the man said. "When the preacher asks if there's anyone there who needs help with a problem, tell him that *you* do. When he asks what your problem is, tell him that you're addicted to drugs and can't stop. You'll see what happens."

The following Sunday, Forrest went to the church in Pontiac, Michigan. He took a seat and listened to the preacher's sermon. When it was finished, the preacher asked, "Is there anyone here who needs help with a problem?"

Forrest stood up and said, "I have a problem."

The preacher asked, "What is your problem?"

Forrest answered, "I take drugs and I can't stop."

Immediately, the entire congregation got up out of their seats and surrounded Forrest in a circle. They embraced him, gave him love, and prayed for him. He never took a drug after that. What people can do when their higher selves are activated is absolutely amazing, and I'll always be grateful to that congregation. Just as an aside, the preacher and the congregation were Black. That is humanity helping humanity. It doesn't matter what color your skin is; we're here to help one another.

Forrest never got married, because he'd made a commitment not to have a child. When any relationship got to the point of being serious, he'd say, "I will not bring a child into this planet, because of the probability that this disease will rear its ugly head. I wouldn't wish this disease on anyone."

Inevitably, he and the woman would break up because she wanted to have a child. His conviction was so strong, that he never changed his mind.

Forrest fell deeply in love five years before he passed away. He met Heather in his favorite bookstore, where she was working. They dated for six months before they became engaged, and they were very happy together. I don't know if he changed his mind about having a child or if she felt the same way. She was lovely, and I was happy for the two of them.

Then tragedy struck. His fiancée died from an overdose. She'd been in rehab, but one night, without Forrest's knowledge, she decided to take drugs. The following morning, he went to her apartment and found her dead. Apparently, Heather had taken the same amount of drugs that she'd tolerated before, but this time that amount killed her, because her system wasn't used to them. Forrest was devastated. It took a huge toll on him, and he never got over it. He had loved her deeply.

I will never know if that incident played a role in Forrest's suicide. He'd been clean for four years and even counseled young people in rehab. He was loved by all of them. They listened to him, because he'd been there. At his memorial, many of them asked me, "He could save *our* lives, so why couldn't he save his own?"

I had no answer.

I think of my son every day. I miss him, but I take solace in the fact that he's in a good place and at peace. That allows me to live in the now and not the past.

Several years ago, I wrote a book called, *Never Saying Goodbye: A Life-Changing Road to Acceptance and Joy After the Loss of a Loved One*. In it, I wrote about the loss of my son and the journey that I took to deal with it. Forrest's passing changed my life drastically. I had to learn to live without him, and at times, I thought I could never do so. Eventually, I took my journey in a different direction that brought me peace and joy. Gerry nurtured me for a full year after Forrest left. I didn't think that I would ever recover, but he was my mast in the storm.

The adage that you cannot completely feel what you have not experienced is true. If people have not had children, they truly cannot feel what a woman who gives birth experiences. If others have not had kidney stone attacks, they cannot imagine the pain that a sufferer has gone through. And if someone has not been discriminated against, he or she cannot understand the agony of being thought of as a second class citizen. But that doesn't mean that we can't help them while they're going through such difficult times.

It took me a year to even try to embark on a new path. It was devastating to wake up every day and know that I wouldn't talk to or see my beloved son again on this planet. There were times when I thought I would never recover. I longed to see him and touch him. I was racked with guilt, as a mother always thinks that it's her fault. I found out through suicide support meetings that I was not responsible. It was difficult for me to acknowledge that, but I finally accepted what I was hearing.

The support-group meetings helped me a lot, and my healing took me into new territory. I ventured to go where I'd never gone before. I wrote my book to help people heal from *any* tragedy that they face. One can live again, and I'm proof that it can happen. My son resides in my heart. He is my spiritual son.

Part of my healing involved joining the Mental Illness Research Association, or MIRA. Gerry and I felt that if we could help prevent one person from taking his or her life, then our mission was successful. I was president for three years and enjoyed every moment of it. I kept thinking of Forrest. We had a research fund at the University of Michigan in honor of him. They discovered that the frontal lobe has a different structure in a person who has bipolar disease, when compared to the brain of a person who does not have bipolar disorder.

Gerry started a program to help young people recognize that they have a brain disease and to prevent them from committing suicide. This program is now in more than 800 schools in the State of Michigan. It has touched thousands of young people.

Suicide is a major cause of death among young people. I received a message on my website from someone who met Forrest years earlier. She had bipolar disease and was addicted to drugs, and she was in a facility to overcome her drug habit. My son had written a raw and riveting poem titled, "Heroin the Omega." This kind, young woman had seen the poem in a magazine and decided to take it to group therapy and read it to all the people there. It was so timely.

I put this poem in my book, *Never Saying Goodbye*, but I feel that it's important to add it here as well. It is raw, and it is heartbreaking. Forrest's pain reverberates throughout. I had no idea what he was going through, because he lived away from home. It's difficult for me to read this poem, and I'm shedding some tears as I type.

I ask myself, "How did this happen?" He was going through such pain, and I, his mother, did not know. This is one of the realities of parenthood; we think all is well with our children, but that is often not the case, particularly when drugs are involved. I know that Forrest hid it from us as long as he could. I found out when he was taking methadone, but I still wonder if I missed the signals before that.

Heroin the Omega

I'm sittin' onna broken
toilet
me
sittin' onna broken toilet
filled with AIDS contaminated
human waste
from hookers n' junkies
me with
roaches
n'
condom n'
filth
at my feet
from

a hundred million
pathetic
fixes and fucks
inna burned out crack
house
near Chalmers n'
Jefferson
tryin'
to git this here 26 gauge
needle
this rusty needleinta the vein
in my groin
you know
into that little hole
I've used so many times
before
you know
the black one
oozing pus n' black
blood
that little hole I've hit so many times
before
you know
you know
the one with the ugly
rash and infection around it
you know the one
and 'm tryin' to feel

good again
like, you know
like I did
so long ago
me hands
me poor hands
me sad ol' hands
is all black n' blue
and swollen
me swollen hands
swollen like boxing
gloves
and so swollen you know
that my crusty fingers
my ugly little fingers
don't work properly
you know
and I'm foolin'
me the fool
me the fool
I'm fooling
with this used rig
I found on the floor
me the fool
me the junky fool
me
the shit goin' solid in the
syringe

And I can't even git a fucking hit

I can't

but it's gonna be alright

you know

cuz I'm gonna git it

together

you know

I'm gonna git it

together

you know

real soon

I am

man I ain't shit in 2

weeks from that fucken

methadone

and I got this case coming up

for dealin'

but my friends in line at

the clinic

bin tellin' me how to

survive in prison

and I got busted again

last week

with a bundle with a

bundle

but it ain't about nothin'

cuz I got a good mouth-

piece

right?
but my veins are all
gone
my blood black veins
all gone
except for what's left of
this one
in my groin
but it ain't working
and I'm bogue as shit
and my lover O.D.'d last week
man
I woke up from a 14
year nod
and she was just a lyin' there
on her back
on her back man
nude, man
there she was nude
onner back
dead stiff n' cold
with this mouth
this gaping mouth
man
this wide open mouth
teeth barred like some
sick demon fangs
with evil foam all over

her face
and man she just turned 23
and I loved her as they
took her out inna black plastic
body gag
(she hated plastic
you know)
but I'm tryin to get off
crap
as I think about how I ripped off
my parents silverware
for this fix
dig
and I'm broke
but it's alright cuz
I'm gonna get it together
next week
ok?
my feet are so swollen
that I cannot tie up
me shoes
and I piss blood
and I can't eat without
pukin'
so I'm liven on
McDonalds milkshakes
but
I know

there's sumptin' bad wrong with my stomach
and my hair's fallin' out
in clumps
my skin is green
and
I need to see a dentist
cuz my teeth are rotten'
but it's cool
cuz I'ma gonna get this hit
this here hit
this one hit
and bang these 4 paks
even tho it ain't working
and I'm tired
I'm sick and tired
I am
tired
So sick n' tired
I'm so fucking sick and tired
and lonely
and alone
And I keep goin' under cuz I'm shootin so
much
dig
even tho the shit ain't getting me off
but I tell you what man
I'll tell you what
I say I'll tell you what

man I'm gonna get it together soon man
I really am
I am
I really am
dig
and it's cool anyway
cuz heroin is so fucking hip

After reading the poem, the young woman told me, "I'd love to meet Forrest."

The woman who was directing the group said, "I know Forrest; I'll call him." And she did, that very day.

The young woman who contacted me said, "I just want you to know that your son spent the entire afternoon talking with me. I think of him every day of my life."

That's the kind of person he was—caring, and wanting to help others. My heart filled with happiness. I will never forget that young woman letting me know what my son had done. I think of her so often.

A few years after Forrest's passing, Gerry ran into a young man at a grocery store who'd been at Forrest's memorial. He approached Gerry and asked, "Aren't you Forrest's stepfather?"

Gerry answered, "Yes."

The young man said, "He saved my life."

Gerry answered, "Yes, I know."

The young man said, "No, you don't. He saved my life. Why couldn't he save his?"

Gerry didn't have an answer for that.

This young man was in the AA program. He told Gerry, "On Sunday night, a memorial is being held for Forrest."

That was two years after Forrest left. I got pleasure from hearing that. My son made an impact by helping people.

I wonder what the common denominator is between all of us on this planet. Is it the capacity to love, hate, survive, self-destruct, cry, attack, help, or ignore? I hope love plays a huge role in all of this. I believe if we can come from love—love for ourselves and others—the world will be a better place.

I remember a famous actress on Broadway who lost her twenty-one-year-old daughter to pneumonia. She was devastated, as was her husband. He kept asking, "Why me? Why me? Why me?"

Finally, the actress said, "Why *not* you?"

That resonated with me. I've learned to accept the realities of life. "Why not me?"

There's an old saying: "I thought it was unfair that I didn't have any shoes, until I saw a man without any feet."

The realities of life can be hard to face, but I've found out that in order to have peace of mind, I must accept these facts of life. It's not easy to do so, but it *is* possible.

My journey has consisted of searching for answers and ultimately finding them. It has taken a long time, but I'm at peace with the hardest reality of them all: losing my beloved son, Forrest, to suicide. I couldn't think straight for a whole year, so I had to learn to live in a new way. I stopped drinking on Forrest's birthday, in honor of him. Because he'd been addicted to drugs, heroin being one of them, I felt that it was important that I not drink anymore. I also started practicing meditation and yoga, which brought peace and acceptance into my life.

I remember going to those suicide support groups after Forrest passed. I was in the depths of pain and sorrow. We all told stories, and one in particular resonated with me. A mother with a now-deceased son said that she was in the kitchen cooking dinner when her thirteen-year-old son told her he was going down to the basement. He'd been there about five minutes when she heard a strange sound coming from down there. She quickly ran down the stairs and screamed when she saw her son lying in a pool of blood. He'd shot himself. I had great compassion for her, and realized that when my own son took his life, I was spared that horrible, gut-wrenching scenario. I knew that as horrible and devastating as my experience was, it could have been worse.

I've devoted many hours trying to help people with brain diseases. They have an illness, not a weakness or character defect. This includes people who live on the street. I don't know why they're there. I only know that they *are*. We shouldn't look *down* at them. We should look directly *at* them. If we truly have love in our hearts, then we can love all of humankind.

Brain diseases are more accepted now, as they should be. There's no difference between someone who has diabetes and some-one who has a brain disease. They're both physical ailments. The only difference is that brain disease is always from the neck up, and there's also a genetic component involved. These sufferers didn't ask for this disease; they were *born* with it, and it can strike at any age, although it usually rears its head in the teen years. People shouldn't carry the burden of shame. It's not their fault.

I respect those who have compassion for humankind, those who truly see all people as worthy, equal human beings. The color of someone's skin or a person's financial worth doesn't enter into those feelings. If there's one thing I've learned on this planet, it's that *we are all equal.*

As the fourteenth Dalai Lama says in his book, *Toward a True Kinship of Faiths: How the World's Religions Can Come Together,*[1] explains that regardless of our wealth, race, education, and spiritual beliefs, all humans desire comfort, happiness, and the best for our loved ones. At the same time, every person experiences pain and joy. It is human and it is universal.

CHAPTER 20

The Loss of My Brothers

Don't make people invalids; let them steer their own course. People should be as independent as they can be, for as long as they can be. Their loved ones should encourage independence… rather than enable dependence.

I visited my brother Tom and his wife, Jan. We had a wonderful time. There were moments of joy and sadness, and I etched them all in my memory bank, because I knew that that this would be the last time I'd see and have worldly contact with my big brother. After spending seven days together, I was ready to leave their house to go back home, and we sadly said our farewells.

The three of us were standing in the vestibule of their home in Studio City, California. Tom and I embraced, and love flowed through us. I could hardly maintain my composure while saying goodbye to him. I would go back to California and visit again, but he wouldn't really be there. His physical body would be present, but not his mind.

That terrible disease, Alzheimer's, had struck Tom four years prior. His mind had been invaded, but a large part of his brain kept him in reality. Five months before my visit, the disease had progressed with a vengeance. Tom, the brother who had loved and protected me my entire life, was slowly ebbing away.

I realize now that I wasn't truly prepared. Before I arrived, I was full of hope that the disease hadn't utterly consumed him. But when I saw him, I was devastated to see that it had taken its toll. I cherished the moments when he knew me, and I took it in stride when he didn't.

At one time, Tom talked to me about dementia and how he would take his own life if it ever descended upon him.

I asked him, "I know that's your decision, but do you know how difficult it is for me to hear you say that?"

He answered, "Yes, I do, but that's how I feel."

I accepted that and hoped that his disease wouldn't progress that far. I was in a dream world, but I just had to keep in mind all of the joy we experienced together. At that moment, the pangs of sorrow were overwhelming, but I knew that the beautiful memories would sustain me. I will always remember all our good times and be grateful that I had such a loving and kind brother for as long as I did.

Tom did pass away twelve months later. One morning, he was doing his two-mile walk, which he'd done for years. Unfortunately, after a short time, the front part of his foot got stuck in the sidewalk. Part of the sidewalk was protruding, because the roots of a tree had grown below it and caused it to change its position. He didn't see that the sidewalk was in that position, so he didn't pick up his feet like he used to before Alzheimer's disease took over his brain. He fell to the ground.

Fortunately, a neighbor was out walking his dog and ran over to Tom when he saw him on the ground. He knew Tom and saw that he was in big trouble. He comforted him and then rushed to Tom and Jan's home to tell Jan, who immediately called 911. Tom was taken to a hospital in Beverly Hills. Blood was flowing from his head, but they didn't know if it was from inside or outside of his brain.

The doctors took many MRIs and decided that it was *not* coming from his brain. But there were other difficulties. Tom couldn't eat any food, so they put a tube down his throat. He wasn't completely lucid, either. There was nothing they could do, and said that he would be on life support for the rest of his life and couldn't return home.

Jan and Tom had agreed that neither of them wanted to be on life support. Jan took the papers that they'd signed to that effect to the hospital. The tubes were taken out, and he lived for a very short time. He was cremated and was finally at peace.

I lost two other brothers, too, and I feel their absence, as I loved them dearly. My brother Jack had cancer and diabetes, and he lost his leg as a result. He was a real trooper and fought that disease with every part of his being. I remember the last time we hugged. I knew that would be our final moment together. I didn't want him to go, but he couldn't continue, because his heart was giving out. He passed the next day.

My brother Kyle was a big part of my life from childhood through adulthood, until he left this planet in 2015 at the age of eighty. Our times together were full of love and tons of fun. Everyone loved Kyle and enjoyed being around him. He just wanted to make people happy.

At the age of seventy-five, Kyle was diagnosed with cancer and heart disease. He suffered for four years and fought valiantly to live. For years, we talked at least once every day, sometimes two or three times. His wife, Darlene, had Alzheimer's, so I knew how lonely his days could be. I was fortunate that we did have wonderful conversations.

Gerry jokingly said, "Kyle is the sister you always wanted."

There was truth in that statement. We talked about anything and everything.

Kyle's health deteriorated drastically from the age of seventy-nine until he passed away at the age of eighty. He fought the battle with all of his determination. At the end of his life while at home, he fell and injured his leg and had to go to rehab. He wasn't happy there and didn't seem to be healing, but we continued to talk every day. After being there for a week and a half, he called me, as he did every day, and said, "Sis, I can't do it anymore."

Previously when he would get depressed from being sick, I was like a cheerleader. I would say, "Yes, you can, Kyle, yes, you can."

This time, I said, "I understand completely. You've fought such a courageous battle, and you've suffered for so long. I understand, and I love you." He was grateful for my reaction.

After being in rehab for two weeks, he took a turn for the worse and was rushed to the hospital. He arrived there on a late Friday night. He called me on Saturday morning and said, "I'm at the hospital, and things aren't going well."

In my heart, I knew that he was ready to leave. We talked for just a few minutes, because I could tell that he was in pain. I got off the phone, and with great sadness and tears, said to Gerry, "I know that Kyle is going to pass today."

A half hour later, the doctor told Kyle, "You're in the process of leaving." The first words out of Kyle's mouth were two jokes. I don't know what they were, but that was vintage Kyle. He always had a great sense of humor, and at times he used it to lighten up dire situations. His doctor had attended to him for 20 years, so it didn't surprise him. Kyle then turned to my brother Jim, who was in Michigan, and said, "Call my sister! Call my sister now!"

When our phone rang, I answered it with a heavy heart, knowing that it was probably Kyle. I knew this would be the last contact I'd have with him on this planet. He and I were both crying while saying goodbye. We kept telling each other how much we loved each other. It was glorious, but it was the saddest phone conversation I've ever had. It is a call that is etched in my memory. I can still hear his voice when I think of him.

I was in Florida, so I couldn't fly in to see him during his last moments. However, I felt fortunate, because we'd flown in for his eightieth birthday on October 9th, 2015. He had five daughters. Mary, his eldest, cooked a delicious dinner for all of us. I sat to the right of Kyle, always my seat when we had dinner at his house.

He kept saying with tears in his eyes, "I'll never see you again."

I said, "No, no, that's not true."

He answered, "Yes, I know it's true."

In my heart full of sadness, I knew there was truth in that statement, but I refused to accept it. I still miss him, but I have glorious memories of our times together. I know how fortunate I was to have had such a close relationship with my brother.

I feel immense gratitude, because I have so many wonderful memories of my brothers. Tom was fifteen months older than I was, and Jack was fifteen months younger. Kyle was four years younger.

I feel there was a certain bond created because of our closeness in age. I feel fortunate to have had those relationships all those years.

My brother Jim is ten years younger than I am. He was born on December 10th, 1941, three days after Pearl Harbor was bombed. I'm grateful that he's still here. He lives in Michigan, and we live in Florida, so we have to talk on the phone. We have great memories and discuss our brothers often. That is comforting to me. I love Jim very much.

I've been fortunate to have had wonderful sisters-in-law: Jan, married to Tom; Carole, married to Jack; Darlene, married to Kyle; and Maida, married to Jim. My nieces and nephews are wonderful as well. Jack and Carole's youngest daughter, Debbi, left this planet four years ago, because she had a brain tumor.

I also have heartfelt memories of my friends who've left this planet. I don't want to sound like a Pollyanna, but if they've suffered and are in pain, then I believe that we should be grateful that life will end for them. I believe our heart tells us that. Are there tearful moments? Yes, but I also like to remember the good, fun times that we had together.

I have a dear friend, Diane Craig, whom I've known since I was nineteen years old, who's in hospice at this moment. She's fought like a Viking for three years, but she's decided that it's just about time to go. I honor that.

We have another friend, Barbara Yearn, and the three of us are very close. At one time, we all lived in Detroit. Now Barbara lives in Michigan, Diane lives in Arizona, and I live in Florida. The three of us had so much fun.

When we were young, we would go to a pub, sit at the bar, order drinks, and wait to see what would happen. Barbara was blonde, Diane was a redhead, and I was a brunette. Just for fun,

Barbara would tell men that her name was Nora and that she was from Norway; she pretended she could barely speak English. Inevitably, a young man or two would come to the bar and ask us if we'd like a drink, and we would accept. Then they'd sit at the bar and start talking to us. They had difficulty talking to Barbara, but they were intrigued and would continue to try to make her understand their English. She would smile and shake her head at them. It was amazing to us that they'd speak English and think they could make her understand. We wouldn't let them order more than one drink, because of the farce that was going on. We were young. As time went on, we didn't do that anymore.

One year later, Barbara was at the pub with her husband. They were sitting at the bar having a conversation. The bartender looked at her and said, "You're amazing."

Barbara asked, "Why?"

He answered, "It's only been a year since I've seen you, but you're already speaking perfect English."

She told him what we'd done, and he thoroughly enjoyed it. That's an example of things that transpired at a young age. We certainly didn't do things like that as we got older. We change as we age. Hopefully we change for the better, as we learn and grow.

As family members and friends leave the planet, I am more and more aware of my own mortality. I miss them and fully realize that my time is also limited here. Realizing that makes my moments here happier and more meaningful. I know that there's always something to learn. This awareness inspires me to live fully each day. I've accepted the losses. I recognize that each day can be emotional and pleasurable, which makes life fuller, and each moment more meaningful. I've learned not to let adversity get in my way.

I also know that my *golden* years have turned out to be my *best* years. True love reigns, and I am so grateful for that.

CHAPTER 21

The Benefits of Being This Age

An oak tree has been steadfast and growing for years. It bends with the wind. It changes its leaves in the fall and provides us with great beauty. It sheds them in the winter and grows new ones in the spring. The shade in the summer keeps us cool. That old oak tree can be relied upon.

The wonderful thing about reaching this age is that I've lived through all the different stages of life so far. I realize that all our experiences can be very different in many ways: how and who we love, how we handled tragedies and illnesses, the depths of depressing times, and the peaks of joy. I've come to understand that each age brings new joys and tragedies. I'm never too old to look at life from a different perspective. That is the beauty of life. The changes don't have to be big; just a small idea is sufficient.

I believe as I travel along the path of life, I become wiser and more understanding. I recognize differences, accept losses, and have the will to continue my life. I'm full of gratitude. I don't yearn for what was; I find pleasure in remembering my walk up until now.

Each step has brought about new thoughts and desires. They're different at this age, but they still come. When I look back, which I don't do often, I recognize that my life was difficult at times, filled with bewilderment and deep sorrow, but I also experienced great happiness.

I know now that what I focus on is what grows. I can't focus on what would have been. I can live life in a direction full of love, compassion, understanding, and acceptance. I have unlocked the door to my own joy.

At times, I felt as though I were in a race against time—so much to do, so much to accomplish. Would it ever get done? I would wake up in the morning with a full agenda and write it all down, checking off each task as I completed it. I could hardly decide what to do first, and confusion reigned. I remember having a toy as a child; it was a top that I could spin instantly. It was spinning, spinning, spinning. I found out that a spinning top stays where it is. Unlike that top, I decided to move forward and not look back. It was one of the most productive things I've ever done.

One of the many benefits of being this age is learning that life is what we make it. There are extenuating circumstances that cause hardships, anger, loss, sickness, and anxiety. But in my own life, I've realized that my role is to accept what appears on my path and then move on. Acceptance allows me to find joy, love, and happiness. I believe in always having a positive attitude. Instead of asking, "Why me?" I ask, "Why not me?"

I've also learned that how I feel is more important than someone else's assessment of me. I don't need acceptance. I don't worry about being judged, and I am not judgmental myself. I go to bed and get up when I want to. I relish each day, and I'm grateful.

We're not clones. My way is good for me, but that doesn't mean that it's good for someone else. I believe that I can live with certain principles. To me, love is the most important ingredient of a happy life. I love myself and I love others. We can be completely different, but we have a connecting thread, and that thread is *life*.

I'm a different person today than I was years ago, and I act accordingly. I've learned so much over the years. That is the beauty of life. Growth is there if we want it. My mindset is very different than it was even five years ago. The road of life has been difficult, harrowing, joyful, and edifying, but I treasure every moment.

At a certain point in life, the memory isn't as sharp as it used to be. The brain computer is full, and it takes a few minutes to get the answer out. When this happens to me, it doesn't mean that I have dementia; it just means that I need to develop a new way of remembering. When I want to recall later where I've put something—for example, my keys—I say to myself, "I'm putting my keys on the dining room table." I assure you that this works. I do it all the time, and it never fails me.

Some people reach a certain age and don't care anymore. Someone may say, "I don't care what people think anymore." That position can have its benefits, unless it's destructive in some way. I can disagree with how someone else thinks and not be rude. I've learned to take other people into consideration. I care about humanity. Some people call it becoming wiser. Hopefully, I've become the ultimate grown-up.

As I've progressed along the path of life, I've come to understand my parents and grandparents better. When I was a child, they were figures of wisdom and parental authority. As I grew, I realized that they didn't know as much as I was led to believe. I found out that they were just human, with all of a human being's fears and anxieties. As I got older, my perception of them changed from authoritative figures to people I considered equals. Understanding people more at this age makes my relationships more meaningful. It is a time of true love. My family and friends have been a huge part of my journey.

I believe that all older people should be viewed as a composite of many ages. They've lived their years accumulating knowledge, experience, and wisdom. Maybe some haven't, but the majority have. They've experienced tragedy, loss, and love. People only see those elders as they are today, instead of realizing that they were babies at one time, then children, young adults, adults, and seniors.

I think that those who have reached their golden years should be respected. People may be retired when they're older, but that only means that they don't work at their careers anymore. They still think, make decisions, and experience sorrow and happiness. They may not have the same physical strength, but they still have emotional strength, love, happiness, caring, awareness, and sorrow. Even when it comes to those who have a hard time walking, I see strength in them, because at least they're trying.

There's a ninety-three-year-old man who lives near us. He walks every morning for two miles. He's bent over and has to stop every five minutes to rest, but he keeps going. He smiles at everyone walking by. They smile back and say, "Hello." He's an inspiration to all of us. People who have that ability are to be cherished.

I wouldn't change my age for any other. I don't yearn for what was; I'm grateful for my bounty. Each step has brought about new thoughts and desires. They may be different at this age, but I still have them. I live one day at a time, and I know that the next moment could be my last. This has been true my entire life, but I have an awareness that has more meaning now.

There really are advantages to being this age. Gerry and I talk about our golden years often, and we enjoy this time. Our desires are different than they were when we were younger. We eat earlier and prefer lunch over dinner. We like to eat healthy food, because we believe it creates a healthy body. We also exercise and practice yoga. We go to bed and get up when we want to.

We've enjoyed all different phases of our lives. We're more grateful for our children, family, and friends. There's an awareness that we're nearing the end of our journeys, and that heightens the pleasure that we get from each day and allows us to live every day fully. There is a peacefulness about having that knowledge.

I try not to waste even one moment. Each one is precious. I'm nearing the end of my road, but I believe that I still have a way to go. What will happen next on my journey? I don't know, but I look forward to it, and I will appreciate every moment of this trip.

I've never been happier. Gerry and I have a glorious relationship, and our children who are still on this planet are content and in good health. If anyone had told me years ago that my life would be as wonderful as it is today, I wouldn't have believed them. Do I wish that my son and my daughter were still here? A quick answer would be "Yes!" Then I realize that they wouldn't be happy living here, and I would not place that burden upon them.

Life does take its turns. I know that my life won't always be smooth sailing, but I accept that and will live one day at a time. I enjoy being in this world. In its totality, I want to be able to say to myself, "You did a good job." It's almost like watching the end of a movie that I've enjoyed very much. I know it's going to end, and I almost don't want it to, but when it does, I know that I'll stand up and applaud.

"I loved it! I did it! I will now be going on to a new adventure!"

There *is* gold in the golden years. Sometimes I've had to dig deep to unearth it, but it's there. It's like discovering gold in a mine. It can be difficult to find, but those nuggets can bring great joy.

There's an old Johnny Mercer song called, "Accentuate the Positive." For me, that's the key to my life. I can do it or not do it. Positive is always better than negative. I'm grateful for all that I've been given. That's my theme in life: *gratitude*. I've experienced some great sorrows, but if I carried them around, it would change how I live today. They're certainly a part of me, but every day I choose to "accentuate the positive and eliminate the negative!"

What Life Has Taught Me

My eyes are staring at the sky. The clouds are big, white, and bouncy. I remember being a child, jumping on the bed and landing on the fluffy pillows. Up and down! Up and down! It was like flying. If only I could fly up to the sky and jump on the pillow in the sky. Childhood beckons at times, but the reality of the present is stronger. A memory bank is good to have, but it's better to live in the now.

I've written down my life story to show how I changed and matured along this road of life and how the final years have their benefits. I understand that some people who are in their golden years are having great difficulties, and my heart goes out to them. I know that this age can be difficult, but it does have its rewards, as all ages do. As I mentioned previously, I'm not a Pollyanna; I accept life on its own terms. Are there bumps in the road? Yes! But I believe in riding over those the bumps, because the road is clear when the bumps are behind us.

My journey wasn't a seamless, guided tour. I made mistakes, but I stand by everything I did. I learned from them and grew from aging. We all make mistakes and do things throughout our lives that we regret. I continue to be aware of that. Will I make more mistakes? I assume that I will. That's part of living. I can look back and say:

"How stupid. Why did I do that?"

But to be healthy, I have to look back and say:

"I know more now than I did then... and I forgive myself."

That equation will continue throughout my life. I don't live in regret; I just go forward.

Our perspectives can change. To keep doing the same negative thing and have the same negative results is detrimental and useless. We need to be open to new ideas. We don't have to participate in them if they don't fit into our psyches. I don't know anyone who can honestly say, "Everything I've done in my life is perfect." All roads can lead us to different destinations. Which one will I choose? That is up to me. I am the driver.

My advice is: Don't be confined. Be free. Don't judge yourself. Be grateful for your life. There will be difficult times and good times. Choose to let the good times come forth. Your perception is your reality. Accept yourself and the life that you've led and are leading. Live your life to learn. Your path is good for you, but that doesn't mean that it's right for someone else. Love is the most important ingredient in a happy life, so love yourself and others.

A feeling of peace came over me when I realized that no one can make me angry. It only happens if I allow it. Have control over what you think, not what someone else thinks about you. The late author Wayne Dyer once said, "What someone thinks about me is none of my business," and that is so true.

Learn to live in the now. Be aware of the present moment, participate in it fully, and be grateful for having that moment, because it will never return again.

Every day is a new beginning. You can make new choices. You can free yourself from past mistakes. Forgive yourself. Take a new path. It takes determination to change one's thinking.

We can pick and choose which memories to focus on. A memory is just a memory, so discard the unpleasant ones, put stars on the joyous ones, and cherish what makes you happy.

Don't judge yourself... or others. We don't know what happened in others' lives to cause them to act or react in the way they do. Be kind to your loved ones and friends by realizing that they may have a right to live the way they want to. Be kind to *everyone*. Forgiving is essential. Direct a smile instead of a frown toward others. Don't condemn yourself, or them.

There can be a lack of compassion for those who are struggling every day and need help. There are people who have to choose between paying their rent or buying their medications. Many people with brain diseases are looked down upon. Some individuals believe that these people are responsible. They're not. These individuals didn't do anything to get that disease. Brain diseases are genetic.

Veterans may find themselves homeless after they've given their all to our country. There are other people who live on the streets for a variety of reasons. They should not be looked down upon. We are here to reach out and help one another. Some people call it becoming wiser.

I remember when our first satellite was sent to outer space in 1958. Most people didn't have a TV to watch that event. They gathered in front of a store window and cheered and clapped their hands at liftoff, when the rocket separated successfully. There was a collective happiness and connection among them. There was pride that the United States of America had accomplished such a great feat. I remember that day so well. Also, I remember when John Glenn became the first man to orbit the earth on November 22nd, 1962. There was immense joy in our country that day.

There was a different reaction on that date one year later, when President John F. Kennedy was assassinated on November 22nd, 1963. This event was viewed on TV, and people were devastated. They were in shock and couldn't understand why this had happened. His widow, Jacqueline, was covered in blood, because she was seated next to her husband in the open motorcade car. She didn't change her clothes or wipe off the blood, because she wanted the public to digest what had happened to her husband, the president.

The nation joined together and mourned. It seemed that everyone had tears in their eyes. It's as though there's a motion picture in my head that gets turned on when I recall certain incidents in history. I suppose it's like going through a photo album, which brings back memories—some happy, some anguish-filled.

America is a different country today than when I was young. There is so much angst and division among people. There are many reasons for that—competing news outlets and social media, to name a few. The government is there to help and protect us, not dictate whom we should love. I feel that there should be separation of church and state. There is *supposed* to be, but some of those protections seem to be slipping away.

I am free. What a wonderful feeling. I can do what I want to do when I want to do it. I don't have the insecurities of youth—that is, having to conform to others' beliefs in order to be liked. Also, I don't follow the trends of fashion anymore; I only did that when I was younger, because I was a fashion model. And I enjoy the music from my younger years. I go to bed and get up when I want to. I relish each day, and I am grateful.

Joy hangs around me like a dear friend. I feel like I've hit the jackpot of happiness. My goal for my journey from now on is solely one of joy, happiness, and gratitude. I didn't always feel this way. For years, it was as if I were living in a vacuum, almost like being programmed. The thought, *What will people think of me?* seemed to dominate me.

Will there now be days of sadness? Yes, but fewer of them. That is the reality. I'm grateful that I'm on this planet surrounded by love. I recognize the privilege of being here. I feel fortunate to have had the experiences I've had. But this is not the end. Every day is a new beginning.

If I sit up in bed and take ten deep breaths, I find that my attitude will change. I can meditate for a few minutes and my mood will improve. My brain influences me and leads my thinking. I can state positive affirmations that enrich my life—for example, "I feel good. Today is a wonderful day. I am grateful for all of the positive elements in my life." (Affirmations are best when stated in the present tense, as if they've already occurred.)

Being healthy has been a very high priority for me. I became quite ill when Forrest and Valarie were young. I went to the doctors at the Osteopathic Hospital in Pontiac, Michigan, and they gave me many tests, but they couldn't determine what illness was causing my problem. Finally, I had a test for hypoglycemia, and it was determined that this was the issue.

It was 1962, and very little was known about hypoglycemia. I had to learn to eat a different way—I had to graze like a cow and monitor my intake of sugar. I attribute my good health at my current age to that experience. I don't take medications, only natural hormones. Also, I've meditated, done yoga, and exercised for thirty years.

What we eat and how we exercise affects our health. A study[2] from Hospital Israelita Albert Einstein in São Paulo, Brazil, suggests a link between regular yoga practice and an increase in brain cortical thickness associated with memory and attention. The researchers found that the cortical thickness in the yoga practitioners was significantly greater in the left prefrontal lobe of the brain. This portion of brain gray matter is linked to awareness, attention, cognitive function, and memory, suggesting that yoga may be associated with cognitive preservation. The scientists said the study confirmed prior reports showing greater gray matter volumes in younger people who practiced yoga and meditation compared to those who did not practice yoga or meditation.

I breathe deeply in and out through my nose when I'm in a stressful situation. Deep breathing creates calmness and better health.

If I don't activate my body, it will get stiff. Doing yoga lubricates my joints. I do this exercise for stability, so I won't get dizzy and fall, which is very important for those who are older. It has been documented that exercise is one of the greatest components in keeping and raising our energy levels. The mind and body need it. Just ten minutes a day makes a difference. I walk outside or on a treadmill, as I've found that an important ingredient to health is moving the body. I recognize that some individuals are limited as to what they can do when it comes to exercise. If someone is in a wheelchair, then their exercises are different. The important issue is to keep moving.

There have been many major advances in science. Some diseases are now treatable. Cancer is not a death sentence, as it was at one time. I remember when people didn't tell others about having cancer, because many thought it was contagious. Psychological diseases are finally being recognized as brain diseases. They're genetic and can be treated. When I was young, people with those diseases were put into institutions. They were drugged and left to die. The movie *One Flew Over the Cuckoo's Nest* was an accurate depiction of what used to go on.

I take fifty minutes per day to meditate, thirty in the morning and twenty in the afternoon. Yoga and meditation have changed my life in a positive way. I've become more introspective and accepting of how people think. My days are much happier as a result of this shifting thought pattern. What I hear and how I exercise affects my health. Yoga and meditation have provided me with great benefits.

If I want to make a delicious dinner, I need to have the right ingredients. If I want to be healthy, I also have to put the right ingredients into my body. To be this age isn't a downer; it's a privilege. I believe in being positive instead of negative. Positive thinking occurred because I reprogrammed my brain in a new direction. I want positive thoughts to vibrate, not negative thoughts. I've learned that I can choose one or the other.

If I don't judge what people do, I am happy. If I forgive everyone, I will be happier. If I live with love, I will be happiest. I believe in being kind to my loved ones and friends by accepting that they can live as they wish to. I believe that forgiveness is essential.

I've come to realize that, in general, we have a tendency to define ourselves by what we *do,* not by who we are. We identify as mother, father, son, daughter, police officer, musician, doctor, teacher, and so on. But that's what we do, not who we are. I believe that I should define myself by how kind, accepting, loving, forgiving, and helpful I am, because that's truly who I am. I've learned that how I feel is more important than someone's assessment of me. As I've said, I don't need acceptance anymore.

As I fill in my birthday calendar, I'm sad that another friend has left, but I'm grateful that this person has been in my life. I cherish my friendships. The memories sustain me. That is the walk of life. The farther along I am on my path, the more my friends tend to leave, but they live in my memory. I can distinctly see them as I think about them. They may not be on this planet physically, but they live in my heart. That's what is so wonderful about the heart. It's never too full to let another memory in.

I'd need four hands to count all of those who've passed. I have four brothers, and three are gone. Life is different without them, and I'm more aware of my own mortality. I wish they could fly down here for a day. We would have a grand reunion. One of the exhilarating times in life is remembering and cherishing those memories.

I think of my son and my daughter every day. I miss them so much, but I take solace in the fact that they're in a good place and at peace. I can recall many tender, loving memories of Forrest and Valarie. I choose to dwell on those, rather than their leaving.

How many times can I say, "I love you"? It is the mother lode for many other feelings: compassion, acceptance, and nonjudgment. I've discovered that they all flow from one place, and the supply of love is limitless. There was an abundance there all the time; all I had to do was find it. This treasure hunt yielded the greatest bounty. Life is short. I want to continue to enjoy it. I want to climb over the obstacles. I can transform fear into love, hate into love, anxiety into love, and confusion into love and clarity. Love is the drug that heals. It is the best ingredient for a happy life.

Usually, we get back what we give out. Positive thinking generates positive actions. So, as you walk your path, try to live with a positive attitude. Negative thinking and negative actions beget negative thinking and negative actions. Take other people into consideration. Be true to yourself, but have consideration for your fellow man and woman.

Look forward, not backward. Don't yearn for what was. Each step brings new thoughts and desires. They're different at this age, but they still come. Forgive yourself for anything you've done in the past that you regret. That just causes anguish. It's over now. Don't let it dwell in your mind. The day you forgive yourself will be your first day of complete freedom and happiness.

I am so grateful that I'm on this planet surrounded by love. I recognize the privilege of being here. I feel fortunate to have had the experiences I've had. But this is not the end. Every day is a new beginning.

The large, white crystal flakes drop gently from the sky and cover the earth below them. The ground looks as if there are diamonds shimmering in the moonlight. I feel grounded and secure. There is a beauty

and quietness about the earth at this moment. All worries, fears, and anxieties lift as I catch one flake with my tongue. It melts immediately. It's like going into a trance of love and warmth. The snow envelops and protects me.

> *The beautiful clouds in the sky look like puffs of cotton.*
> *They have the freedom to change from minute to minute.*
> *We all have the same freedom. Don't get stuck in one*
> *place. Be open to new ideas.*

About the Author

Mary Jean Teachman was born in Detroit, Michigan, to Isabelle and George Dresbach. She attended the University of Detroit, where she studied prelaw and mathematics. She married and had two children, Arthur Forrest Tull and Valarie Tull. She later divorced, was single for four years, married Mort Lieberman, and after eighteen years of marriage, was widowed.

Mary Jean found love again with Gerard Teachman, PhD, and inherited two wonderful sons, Robert and Jonathan; she and Gerry have been married for thirty-two years. She had a very successful career for eight years as a runway and print model, and she appeared in *Vogue* magazine.

A longtime activist, she started a successful campaign—"Real Americans Buy American Cars" (RABAC)—in the late 1970s. She started this grassroots movement because the American auto industry was in a severe slump. Her idea was to help convince the American public to support American car companies in their struggle against foreign imports, and save jobs in the process. She distributed bumper stickers and gave interviews to the print and broadcast media. At one point, a representative from the Japanese government came to interview her, because they felt threatened by this movement. Gradually, the unions adopted the project, which developed into their "Buy American" campaign.

Mary Jean was president of Groesback Investments for three years and a board member for ten. In Palm Beach Gardens, Florida, she sits on the board of the John E. Upledger Foundation, an international healthcare resource center that is recognized worldwide for its comprehensive education programs, advanced treatment options, and unique outreach initiatives. She was also president of the Juno Beach Chapter of the Florida Shore and Beach Renourishment project in the early 1990s. She was president of her homeowner's board in Juno Beach, Florida, and has been active in numerous charities. She has also served as a chairperson for many charitable events.

Mary Jean's past hobbies have included being an avid gardener, a gourmet cook, and an investor, but her primary interest has been her family. She and her husband reside in Juno Beach, Florida, and Asheville, North Carolina. She is ninety-one, and considers it a privilege to have reached this age. She is now looking forward to being 100 years old.

Endnotes

1   The Dalai Lama, Toward a True Kinship of Faiths: How the World's Religions Can Come Together (New York: Harmony, 2011).

2   Afonso, Rui F. et al. "Greater Cortical Thickness in Elderly Female Yoga Practitioners – A Cross-Sectional Study," National Library of Medicine (2017), https://www.ncbi.nlm.nih.gov/pmc/articles/PMC5476728/.